To: Louise and Gerry

JAMES H. CRITCHFIELD

His Life's Story 1917 – 2003

With All Best Wishes,

Lois M. Critchfield

Lois

authorHOUSE®

AuthorHouse™
1663 Liberty Drive
Bloomington, IN 47403
www.authorhouse.com
Phone: 1 (800) 839-8640

Published by AuthorHouse 12/21/2018

ISBN: 978-1-5462-6977-9 (sc)
ISBN: 978-1-5462-7453-7 (hc)
ISBN: 978-1-5462-6975-5 (e)

Library of Congress Control Number: 2018913930

Printed in the United States of America.

PREFACE

This is a very personal story written for family and friends, but it is also a kind of role model for young people who wonder why some are selected out for special admiration and respect. I had put Jim Critchfield in that category long before we were married. I started this memoir in 1995 and am just now finishing it. I am finally letting it see the light of day. But before I begin, let me share with you the eulogy given by grandson Daniel Webster. It beautifully describes this extraordinary man.

James H. Critchfield—May 23, 2003,
Fort Myer Old Chapel

He was so many things to so many people here today.

A husband, a father, a brother, a companion, ein guter freund Deutschlands, a neighbor, mentor, and confidant. And a grandfather. And like so many other things in his life, he did that very well.

His life spanned some of the greatest changes our nation and our world have ever seen. The Great Depression, the fiercest war ever fought, the Cold War with the rise and fall of the Soviet Empire, the dawning of the nuclear age, and staggering advances in technology, and communications, energy, and transportation.

Had Ian Fleming and Rudyard Kipling ever collaborated, I doubt they would have created a character such as him or a story with so much.

From literally a little house on the prairie to our nation's capital, from hay harvesting with steam engines on farms in the flat fertile Midwest to the Black Forest of Germany. As he termed it, his great adventures led him to the Mexican border, to North Africa, Europe, and the tumultuous Middle East across the globe to where the Himalayas touch the sky.

From some of the bloodiest battles in Europe, to quiet walks beside the Atlantic Ocean in the Outer Banks, a place called Scuffleburg in the Blue Ridge Mountains, revived under his watchful touch.

From endless fields without fences, to a wall in Berlin, an Iron Curtain, and a stone wall built by his hands on a wandering country lane.

He was a true US Cavalry horse soldier, a Buffalo Soldier, and earned the Purple Heart, a Silver Star, several Bronze Stars, and the rank of colonel ... all by the age of thirty.

He was recognized for his contributions by the Central Intelligence Agency, North Dakota State University, the Sultanate of Oman, and the Republic of Germany.

He has been called a spymaster, and I can tell you he sort of spied on things all his life. For to spy can be defined as to observe, listen in, look upon, and reflect. He would listen with such an active and engaging intensity. Anyone who spent any time with him felt the connection by his conversation with him.

He did this his whole life with such an avid interest in all manner of things in the world about him.

He shared with me his own observation about becoming the man he was and his marriage.

He wrote me:

> It was not until I was much older and more exposed to life that I began to remember all the little occasions when I might have been more thoughtful, more sensitive and more considerate. How good it would be if some of the wisdom of later years could be acquired in youth. I am deeply impressed as each day passes at the number of loving and considerate acts that are a part of the mature marriage that Lois and I have achieved. We still view it with some wonder. But it is not a matter of magic; we also work at it every day and share the joy of doing so.

He listened and reflected upon his own life often, and through that he became the grand, gracious, and gallant man he was.

Franklin Delano Roosevelt said my grandfather's generation of Americans had a rendezvous with destiny. And Tom Brokaw dubbed them the Greatest Generation.

Well we here are the fortunate ones, for we are blessed to live in a world that is a direct result of the sacrifice, honor, and courage of men like James Critchfield and their rendezvous with destiny.

And I know that he will look in and spy a bit on us all from time to time.

PROLOGUE

Born to Mr. and Mrs. R. J. Critchfield Tuesday, January 30,
a baby boy
Hunter Herald
February 8, 1917

James Hardesty Critchfield, the first boy and the second
child of Jim and Ann Critchfield, was born on the family
farm about two miles outside of Hunter, North Dakota.
Hunter is some forty miles north and slightly west of Fargo.
Today it consists mainly of three huge grain elevators by a
rail line, a few shops, churches, and small homes. It is now
a mere cog in the current world of agribusiness, and during
Jim's last visit there in the late 1980s, he thought it looked
more like an American version of a Soviet collective farm.

Both grandmothers were there when Jim was born.
Jessie Williams from Iowa and Lillie Critchfield, who lived
in the big house in town built by her husband, Henry, who
had died fifteen years earlier. Dr. W. V. Baillie, who had
taken over Henry Critchfield's medical practice, delivered
the baby.

Hunter was also the birthplace of Jim's father. Both
father and grandfather were country doctors, who over the
years made thousands of house calls by horse and buggy
to treat hundreds of patients at neighboring farms. When
they were not doctoring, they were farming. This partially
explains Jim's love of the farm and horses, and for most of
his life, he continued to diagnose his own illnesses while
prudently obtaining second opinions from modern medical
specialists.

Jim's grandfather, Dr. Henry Critchfield, was born in
Millersburg, Ohio, on May 20, 1861. He went to the Dakota
Indian Territory in the 1880s, where he spent the rest of
his life as a country doctor. According to the *Record*, vol.
1, no. 7, published in Fargo in 1895, Dr. Henry Critchfield

"enjoyed an exceptionally large practice and in the past two years has ridden over 200,000 miles." In 1904, returning one night from a call, his horses led him into a deep water hole. He could not get the team and buggy out, so he unhitched the team and walked a long way to a farmhouse. He became ill with pneumonia and died in Minneapolis within a few days. He was only forty-three years of age.

Dr. Henry Hardesty Critchfield and fourteen-year-old son Ralph James in front of their home in Hunter, North Dakota, in 1903

BOYHOOD

Mother with Jim and Betty

Jim's boyhood years were spent in Hunter, Maddock, and Fessenden, all small Dakota towns. He and his older sister Betty also had tastes of less rugged life in Iowa, their mother's former home. Ann frequently bundled up the children and drove to Iowa over dirt and gravel roads for family visits. When Jim Sr. was going to medical school in Minneapolis, Ann took the two children home to Iowa. To help pay for their added expenses, she taught school in Viola, and the family lived in the Methodist parsonage. But by 1922, Jim Sr. had completed his internship in Minneapolis and accepted an offer to open a practice in Maddock, a small town farther west in the prairie, which was predominantly Scandinavian. The family lived three years in Maddock and then moved to Fessenden, the county seat of the adjacent Wells County, thirty miles away. While the family lived in Maddock and Fessenden, the final three children were born: Bill in 1923, Peggy in 1929, and Pat in 1931. All were born in Minneapolis. Jim Sr.'s brother Ray, also a doctor, was there, and they felt it was safer for Ann.

For Jim and sister Betty, life both in Maddock and Fessenden was full of delights. Their father, exuding good humor and with never-ending energy, was a town leader, organizing band concerts, musicales, and parades. Holidays were festive occasions with many friends and neighbors taking part. Christmas, with horses and sleighs; Fourth of July; and the county fair were among the big events the children looked forward to each year. It was an age of innocence for the children, who could go anywhere around town and in the countryside without fear.

Jens Nielsen, a Danish immigrant who farmed the land near where the Critchfields lived in Maddock, came to be one of the major influences in Jim's early life. Jens was a good friend of his father; they played poker together, always gambling, if not for very high stakes, and a bottle of schnapps was ever present. Jim described Jens during an interview for *Those Days*:[1] "He had black hair, mustache, red cheeks, and chewed Copenhagen snuse. He was never in such a hurry that he would not stop, pause to show me and explain to me why things were done the way they were." Jens loved horses. He had a stable of draft horses, produced by mustang mares bred to imported European stallions. Jens introduced Jim to the world of horses— how to break them and how to care for them. He had a blacksmith shop with forges, a harness shop, and a general tool shop. To young Jim, age ten, this was exciting stuff.

Jim Sr. arranged with Jens to teach Jim the basic elements of growing and harvesting wheat. At age ten, Jim was in charge of the water wagon, delivering water by horse-drawn tank to the massive steam engine that powered the huge forty-four-inch Case threshing machine. By age fifteen, he was promoted and earned a full man's wage—five dollars a day—to work in the fields harvesting and threshing. Living with the itinerant workers in the bunkhouse, Jim also got a full education in some raw realities of life as lived by those lusty workers. Even after the family moved to Fargo, Jim would return to work at the Nielsen farm during school vacations. Unquestionably, Jens Nielsen was a major factor in the transition of Jim from childhood to adolescence. He worked with him during the good times but also the hard times, such as the grasshopper attacks and the dust bowl, which demolished Jens's crop and land. Finally in 1934, walking with Jens over his land, which was laid bare by wind, dust, and Russian thistles, and hearing the despair in Jens's voice, Jim realized that the end of farming as he knew it was near. Although Jens picked himself up and continued farming, it was never the same. Before long, farming became mechanized, and the horse was sidelined. But the experience left an indelible impression on young Jim Critchfield.

During the same period in Jim's life, he was also influenced greatly by the Iowa relatives. Given Jim's mother's proclivity for travel, driving back and forth to Iowa became a ritual everyone loved. Jim's visits there also involved farming, as well as many Methodist church socials and visits to Quaker relatives in nearby Mount Vernon, a more austere group of cousins in Jim's opinion. While in Iowa, Jim's uncles Fay and Victor Collins took him in hand and taught him their style of farming. So between raising ginseng and haying in Iowa and threshing in North Dakota, by the time school started in the fall, Jim had a well-rounded education in farming techniques.

HIGH SCHOOL DAYS

The move to Fargo in 1932 marked a turning point in Jim's life. His father decided to move to the city and open an office downtown. It was a major move for this fifteen-year-old who had only known small-town life. According to his own words, he was terribly shy and embarrassed when meeting new people and yearned to be back in Maddock and Fessenden. He even tells of being sick with yellow jaundice in the spring of his first year in Fargo, causing him to be out of school for almost two months. Upon returning to school, nobody noticed that he had been away. Now, that made him mad. And that anger contributed to making him an achiever.

But he was not totally a self-starter. He will be the first to give credit to a group of girls who apparently had noticed him and decided to become his silent supporters. He was then in his junior year at Fargo Central High School. He started getting invited to parties, the most important of which was the one where he met Connie Taylor. Then there were the dances. The girls, Connie, LaVaun Anderson, and Maxine Schollander, among others, would plan who would dance with whom, and they would even fill out the dance cards. Those were the days of the fox trot, waltz, Charleston, and the big apple. The boys never knew until they got to the dance what would be going on. But the last dance was always with Connie.

Jim's best friend throughout his high school years was Ross Porter. They were back and forth at each other's homes. They were deep into sports, from football to tennis. Life had suddenly become very busy.

One of his most supportive friends was Herschel Lescowitz. Herschel lived in the more fashionable south side of Fargo and was active in school affairs. He went on in later life to be mayor of Fargo for many consecutive terms. One day late during their senior year, Herschel took Jim aside and said, "Jim, I am going to support you for 'Representative Senior.'" That was the high school's most prestigious award. "I would like to have the award myself, but I know I can never make it." Herschel was Jewish and a distinct minority in Fargo. It never occurred to this farm boy from the prairie that being Jewish carried a stigma.

He tucked that thought away for further consideration. Later on, at the General Assembly, when it was announced that Jim had been named the most 'Representative Senior,' he was just as surprised as if he had never heard of the suggestion. For having entered Fargo High School as a somewhat poorly clad, shy adolescent, he graduated from it with distinction and a bit more self-confidence.

But it was not a foregone conclusion that Jim would go on to college. The family situation had deteriorated considerably. Jim's father's medical practice was not doing well; he showed little interest in his children, his marriage was at its lowest ebb, he was drinking too much, and money was tight. Betty had dropped out of college in order to contribute to the family finances. Ann and the three children took off for Iowa, and all in all it was a sad situation. Jim stayed with Ross Porter after graduation and wondered what he should do. Jim Sr. told him to get a job and become the family breadwinner.

And then something happened, another little episode in his walk through life, which left an impact. Uncle Burke Critchfield, Jim Sr.'s brother and then a vice president of the Bank of America in San Francisco, had just bought back the family farm near Hunter where Betty and Jim had been born. He wanted to restore it. He offered Jim the job, the use of a 1933 Ford coupe, and $150 upon completion. Jim took off for Hunter and a period of backbreaking work and solitary reflection. He slept at his Grandmother Lillie's home in Hunter, and that was his only social contact. During this time, he spent many hours thinking about what to do about the future.

During the summer months, he repaired and painted all the farm buildings, most of which were just short of collapse. They were painted red with white trim. As for the main house, Burke wanted a new cellar dug (the old house was only sitting on a root cellar) and the house moved a few hundred yards to this new location. Then the house

5

was to be repaired and painted white. Jim worked totally by himself. I think this instilled in him a great sense of self-reliance. So many examples come to mind of projects he has done throughout the years where he did the whole thing himself, whether it was building and repair projects, planning military strategy, or writing a five-year plan for the Oman Petroleum Ministry. He simply preferred to do it himself.

Even if it had occurred to him, he had no money to hire additional help at the farm. Day after day, he hauled, lifted, repaired, and painted. As for the cellar, he used a team of horses and a large metal shovel called a slip and started digging a hole the size of the house. When it came time to move the house, he finally called in assistance. Mr. Timmerman, a retired bridge builder from the nearby town of Arthur, came with his equipment. They jacked up the house, and the two of them put bridge timbers under it and pushed it with ratchet jacks, slowly easing it onto the new foundation. It worked!

By now, the summer was almost over. Ann and children were back from Iowa, and Jim drove into Fargo to buy more paint. He still didn't know what the future would hold. With every intention of finishing the job at Hunter, once in Fargo he found all of his friends excitedly enrolling at the Agriculture College (AC), as it was then called; it is now North Dakota State University. He got caught up in their enthusiasm and said to himself, *I can make it.* He had enough money for tuition ($17 per semester) and was invited to join the Alpha Tau Omega fraternity, which would waive the initiation fee if he would clean all the bathrooms and do other menial chores. Jim was later to become president of the chapter.

As for the restoration job, Burke only paid him $75 of the $150 he owed him. Many years later, Jim and Burke, then president of the California Wine Growers Association, were on a tour of vineyards in Germany and France. Jim reminded Burke he had never met his commitment for that summer's work. Burke professed not to believe it, but for the next three days in Paris, he picked up the hotel tab and other expenses.

COLLEGE DAYS

The four years at North Dakota Agricultural College (NDAC) were happy ones for Jim despite the fact he had no money; he rushed from one part-time job to another and took a maximum load of courses. He doesn't recall that this interfered at all with the many extracurricular activities in which he was involved.

He worked his jobs in between classes and other activities. Half a block from the fraternity house was the Dutch Kitchen where each day he peeled a half-bushel of potatoes and once a week scrubbed the floors. He ran a hatcheck booth at the bowling alley downtown. (This actually was a scholarship from the bowling alley to the top athlete at the fraternity house, a football player who sublet the concession to Jim, who under the agreement took a portion of the proceeds for himself.) He did some work for the *Fargo Forum*, his first real job, which was to read the obituaries of the local North Dakota papers and extract items of interest. In his third year, Jim became editor of the NDAC yearbook, *The Bison*, a paying job at $20 a month. That really took the pressure off him financially.

When Jim started at NDAC, he signed up for engineering, but his interest in English, history, and the social sciences sidetracked him. A look at his transcript included here shows an amazing picture. First, by the time he graduated he had completed 210 credit hours, or thirty-five hours per semester. He took every English course the school offered and most of the history, economics, and political science courses. The problem was that when graduation time came,

7

he had not completed the needed courses for a degree in engineering. The faculty, somewhat culpable for not seeing this before his last year, worked out a schedule of what classes he simply had to have on his record to graduate. Jim hunkered down that last year and completed them. He got his bachelor of science degree, but he also got a well-rounded education in the liberal arts.

The rest of the Critchfields lived only a block from campus. Betty was still working but would start back to college during Jim's senior year. Ann, not at all atypical of her nature, became sort of an off-campus housemother. Jim's classmates would gather there for hot chocolate and sweet rolls fresh out of the oven, and they would talk about all the issues of the day. There would be readings from plays, good books, and poetry. One of Jim's close friends, Mike Hurdlebrink, an amateur poet, would read his latest. Mike went on to become president of Martin Senour Paint Company and a trustee of the Colonial Williamsburg Foundation.

The most important person at those gatherings was Leon Hartwell, an import from the more aristocratic Eastern establishment, who taught all the interesting literature classes at NDAC. Hartwell intrigued his students with his somewhat mysterious background. He told them of the time when he was living in Budapest, and in despair over a lost love or what he considered a wasted life, he stood in the middle of the bridge connecting Buda and Pest and considered flinging himself off into the murky river below. The only reason he did not was a letter in his pocket from NDAC offering him a teaching position. He figured the prairie college could not be any worse than death in the Danube River. Hartwell had a big impact on his students, and they apparently had a positive influence on him. Although Jim lost track of him after college, he found many years later that Hartwell, then in his eighties, was living in a veteran's retirement facility in Portsmouth, Virginia. It is believed that when World War II came along, Hartwell joined up and then afterward settled back in his home territory of New England. Unfortunately, Hartwell was afflicted with Alzheimer's disease, making any reunion impossible.

There was also a lighter side to life at school. In addition to the more classical gatherings at the Critchfield home, the crowd would also meet at the Tower Coffee Shop in downtown Fargo near the Fargo Theater. A waitress there, Peggy Lee (born Norma Egstrom), was a favorite of Jim's fraternity brothers and sang all the songs of the day, such as "Deep Purple," "Stardust," and, of course, the "Sweetheart of ATO." Jim's fraternity brothers kept trying to raise funds so that Peggy could go to NDAC, but they were never able to get quite enough. As it turned out, she did quite well on her own. She performed well into the 1990s, and her records, of course, are legendary.

Connie and Jim were a twosome all during this period. Neither one of them had committed to a life together, but it was understood. When Jim was editor of *The Bison* in 1939, Connie was coeditor. When Captain James Critchfield commanded the ROTC Company A, Connie was the company sponsor. Jim was a member of Scabbard and Blade, the honorary fraternity for ROTC officers, and Connie was a member of Guidon, the auxiliary to Scabbard and Blade. During his senior year, Jim was also the president of the Student Commission and in charge of organizing student events, the biggest of which was the annual homecoming parade and game festivities. Connie was gracious when Jim deserted her to perform his "duty" of escorting Homecoming Queen Claire Putz onto the playing field at halftime.

Jim was twenty-one years old and a junior at NDAC when his father died. Jim Sr. had been ill for more than a year. He had reunited with Ann and the family, but it was not long before he was hospitalized, first in Minneapolis and then for the last six months of his life at the Veterans Hospital in Fargo and St. Cloud, Minnesota. Ann was with him every day, and while Jim Sr. was in the hospital in

Fargo, the children would go to see him. But it is one of the puzzles of Jim's life why he was the only one of the family who did not go to the hospital. It may have been a sense of bitterness that his father was not ambitious for him and didn't recognize his various accomplishments and that he was forced to go out on his own to carve out his future. The few times he saw his father before he quit his medical practice were not very pleasant. It seems that the two grew apart, and Jim went on with his own life.

If one were to predict the direction of Jim's future in 1939, they would probably say that he would go into journalism or the publishing business. And that almost happened. But it turned out to be the military track instead. And in a sense, that was almost accidental. Once before, Jim had a military career dangled before him. In 1935, his uncle Ray, by then a successful physician in St. Paul, wrote to him offering to help him with a West Point appointment. Jim never followed up. At the time Jim attended NDAC, basic ROTC was a requirement for all boys. He went through the program but did not, however, take the next step and apply for advanced ROTC, which would give him an automatic reserve commission in the United States Army and would virtually point him in the direction of a military career.

One day out of the blue, a fraternity brother, Cadet Colonel Francis "Frog" LaMarre, who was two years ahead of Jim, told him that one of the cadet officers broke his leg and had to drop out of the program. He offered to recommend Jim as this man's replacement, and, after the required interviews, Jim found himself in the advanced ROTC program headed for the reserve commission. And not only that, he was paid a small stipend for participating. Jim commented much later that this training was first class, and he applied much of it during duty with the US Army in World War II. He said some of his West Point friends felt that the ROTC program surpassed the training they had received at the Point. One friend remarked, "They train you to be generals at West Point, not how to fight wars."

So the four years sped by. The NDAC yearbook tells it all:

James Critchfield—Applied Arts and Sciences

Alpha Tau Omega, President and Vice Pres; Blue Key; Scabbard and Blade; Pres of the Student Commission; Bison Editor '38 and '39 Bison Sports Editor; Asst Business Manager, The Spectrum; Pres, Intramural Athletic Board Freshman Class President; VP of North Central Press Conference; Freshman and Sophomore Class Plays; Blue Key Scholarship; Thomas Arkly Clark Award; Captain, ROTC; YMCA Cabinet; Intramural Hockey and Basketball; Interfraternity Council

When Jim left NDAC, he never looked back—well, at least not for forty-seven years. In 1986, he was awarded an honorary doctor of science from North Dakota State University, the former NDAC. At the same time, Richard Patrick "Brother Pat" Critchfield, by then an award-winning journalist, received an honorary doctor of humane letters. It was a great occasion with many family members in attendance.

But hold on! A year later, the National Association of State Universities and Land Grant Colleges chose Jim to represent NDSU as its Centennial Alumnus. Only one alumnus was selected from each of the nation's 149 universities from among many candidates nominated. After the awards ceremony in Washington to celebrate the one hundred years of land grant college education, Jim returned to Fargo to be recognized by NDSU at its 1988 commencement. Typically, Jim felt there were many NDSU alumni more deserving of this honor. It was a humbling experience. And in acceptance of both honors, he gave full credit for the successes he had to growing up and being educated in North Dakota.

DAYS OF THE HORSE CAVALRY

College was over, and Jim headed for a job in the US Army, having chosen this over an $18 a week job offer by the Boone County, Iowa, *Messenger*, a job that involved not only newspaper writing but also working on makeup and selling advertising. The US Army pay would be $20 a week and seemed to hold out more promise. The army at the time was operating under the Honor Graduate Act of 1922, which called for candidates to fill the spots that would normally be filled by West Point graduates, because West Point was not graduating enough men to staff the army.

By sleight of hand, some would say, Second Lieutenant James H. Critchfield during the summer of 1939 reported to the Fourth US Cavalry at Fort Meade, South Dakota. Given the type of training he had received at the advanced ROTC, he should have gone to an infantry unit, but Arthur R. Lacey, who headed the visiting board that interviewed candidates for regular commissions, after talking with Jim for a period of time, scratched out infantry and wrote in cavalry. The ROTC instructors were not too happy about that, but it was out of their hands. It was yet another example of fate intervening to reset the course of life. In 1878, the Sioux Indians had established Fort Meade, once known as the Peace Keeper Post on the Dakota Frontier, to protect the white settlers from attacks. Until the mechanization of the cavalry, it was for most of its sixty-six-year history home to the horse soldiers.

Shortly after arriving at Fort Meade, one Captain Lewis B. Rapp, a regular army officer who had spent seventeen years as a first lieutenant, stopped by to welcome Jim to the officer corps of the US Cavalry and to pass on some seasoned advice:

1. Always pay your debts.
2. In the army, one goes to chapel, not to a specific church.
3. Don't join a political party.
4. Don't have anything to do with any woman that lives within two miles of the flagpole.
5. Stay single so that you can piss on the fire, whistle for your dog, and get on your horse and leave.
6. To get ahead, get assigned to a headquarters, always walk briskly, and carry papers in your hand.

Connie stayed on at the AC for another year to complete a few more courses and to be the editor of *The Bison* yearbook. In the meantime, Jim's days were spent on maneuvers in Arkansas, east Texas, and Louisiana. The horses were shipped down to the area by boxcar. It was during this time that the German attack on France occurred. And more and more, people were discussing the question of whether the United States should or should not go to war.

Then a shocking thing happened. One day in the spring of 1940, half of the Fourth Cavalry troops from Fort Meade found themselves suddenly without horses. Washington had made the decision to mechanize and assign these horse soldiers to half-tracks and motorcycles. Orders were to turn the horses in to the quartermaster in Texas, learn to drive the Harley Davidsons, and proceed back to Fort Meade. They were stunned. Jim's assignment was to get those Harley Davidsons up and running, and, after a quick checkout with the company rep and the manual in his back pocket, he and his troops headed back. It was humiliating but at the same time exciting. Who could resist the glamour of riding down the highway with the wind blowing on either side of you as you took those forty-five-degree turns heading out of Texas back to the Great Plains? Most of the men adapted, but some had to make the trip by sidecar. And only a few of the cycles burned out their engines on the way.

But Jim soon got back to horses. He was assigned to take the officers' course at the Cavalry School at Fort Riley, Kansas. After that, he took the communications (Morse code) course there. But before leaving for Kansas, he went back home, and on September 25, 1940, he and Connie Taylor were married. His good friend Ross Porter was best man, and Betty was the maid of honor. The long-awaited event took place at the United Methodist Church with the reception there afterward. It was a happy occasion, as would be the following months. The idea of the United States entering the war was still a matter of debate.

Then Jim's career reached a turning point. While at Fort Riley, he was asked if he would become the regimental communications officer of the recently reassembled Tenth Cavalry, part of the Second Cavalry Division. His response was that he would do whatever was in the interest of the service. Now what he had not known is that he could have turned that down and gone back to the Fourth Cavalry, and it would not in any way adversely affect his record. In fact, he thinks he was expected to turn it down. For, you see, the newly reactivated Tenth Cavalry was, except for the officer corps, made up entirely of black troops. It was odd to learn of the negative reaction of the powers-that-be back in Fort Meade. For example, a Fourth Cavalry tradition for newly married officers was to give the couple an engraved silver bowl. The Critchfields' bowl had been engraved and was waiting for presentation. When Jim accepted the Tenth Cavalry assignment, the Fourth Cavalry executive officer issued instructions to return the engraved silver bowl to the manufacturer.

Indeed, this was still a time of huge divisions between the black and white populations in the United States. As one black officer said recently, there were two armies in the United States, a white one and a black one. The silver bowl episode was Jim's first exposure to a subtle version of the discrimination that existed among the military services at the time. Having been raised in North Dakota against the traditions of the Great Plains, he had, prior to the assignment to the Tenth Cavalry, virtually no contact with those who today are described as Afro-Americans. As it turned out, he served with the Tenth Cavalry from 1941 to early 1944 when it was deactivated in North Africa. He thinks he may be the only officer to go from the rank of second lieutenant to lieutenant colonel with this regiment.

It was a great experience. The Tenth Cavalry actually was a historic military unit. Formed at Fort Leavenworth in 1866 of "colored volunteers," the Tenth patrolled the West and Southwest protecting the white pioneers against the Indians, who were desperately trying to hold on to their hunting lands. The troopers were known as the "Brown Buffaloes." They fought Geronimo, chased the Apache Kid, pursued Pancho Villa deep into Mexico, and stormed San Juan Hill with Teddy Roosevelt. One of its more famous officers was General John J. Pershing, who had been a first lieutenant with the regiment. In 1931, the Tenth Cavalry was split up; parts went to West Point and parts to Fort Myer and elsewhere. But in February 1941, the entire regiment was reassembled and assigned to Camp Funston, which was adjacent to Fort Riley. It had 1,326 men and 1,280 horses. And the regiment needed a communications officer.

Jim's first assignment was to form a platoon and train it to operate radios. In the beginning, he had Master Sergeant Watkins and one private and no radios. But before long, he was able to bring the platoon up to strength when most of a big band from Kansas City enlisted en masse at Fort Leavenworth with the agreement they would accept any assignment other than the regimental band. Those jazz musicians made marvelous radio operators and took no time in learning Morse code. They even good-humoredly accepted the rules of military discipline. In the off hours there was great music; the group carried a piano around with them in a truck.

Life at Fort Riley was great. Housing was a bit tight at first. Connie and Jim shared a house at Junction City with Lieutenant Kimo and Jane Ellen Dunn, also from the Fourth Cavalry, also newlyweds. The owners from whom they rented lived in the basement. It was tight quarters, but everyone got along, it appears. Kimo went back to the Fourth Cavalry and, two hours before H Hour on D-Day, landed in France off Utah Beach. After the war, he continued his army career and eventually retired in San Antonio with the rank of major general. Fifty years later, Kimo wrote Jim reminiscing about those early days.

Pearl Harbor happened, as we know, on December 7, 1941. And then the momentum began to pick up with intensive and sustained training programs. During the spring of 1942, Jim, who by then was the commander of the Second Squadron, along with the entire Tenth Cavalry, moved to Camp Lockett, California, on the Mexican border.

There were weeks of field exercises along the border and maneuvers in Louisiana and east Texas with the First Cavalry Division and other infantry, artillery, and cavalry units. Jim was proud of the performance of his troopers, who in spite of the disadvantages of segregation, performed with much pride and esprit.

During his time at Camp Lockett, Jim kept in touch with his mother, Ann, by mail. In one letter that has survived the years, he made these poignant remarks about his early years.

Oh, Mom—I never appreciated my childhood until I grew up. A million and one things that I have always considered just "normal" did so much to form all the ideas I have. When Connie and I have a family, we are going to do all the things that our family did—lots of pomp and ceremony at Christmas and Thanksgiving, give the kids books like *Little Men* and *Little Women* and all the million and one things that made up our life at the Critchfield house. You built up a truly wonderful home, Mother, and I will never be able to repay you—I do not see how boys and girls coming from your house could help but be good people.

The timing of this letter can probably be explained because they were expecting their first child. Connie stayed in Fort Riley as the baby was due in the summer of 1942. Camp Lockett was set up for dependents only after they were born. Michel Ann arrived on July 15, and as soon as they could travel, Connie and Ann (Mikey) joined Jim on the Mexican border. While the officers and men at Camp Lockett knew they would eventually be joining their brothers in the war, that did not deter them from making the most of what Camp Lockett had to offer. It was a society built around horses. There were polo matches, horse-jumping events, trail rides, lots of parties, and picnics. Officers even competed in polo matches with civilian polo groups in San Diego and Los Angeles.

Major Critchfield on Saad (Arabian horse—
Saad means *happiness* in Arabic) in 1942 at
Camp Lockett, where the Tenth Cavalry Buffalo
Soldiers trained for combat in Europe

But it was inevitable that the call would come, and late in 1943, the Tenth Cavalry as a regiment received orders to move out. They were to report to Hampton Roads in Virginia to embark for North Africa. And they were to report without horses. The Quartermaster Remount Service arrived and once again took away all the horses. Although the crossed sabers continued to be the insignia for the Tenth, there would be added to it now the emblem of a tank. For the Tenth Cavalry, this was the end of the horse era. It had been happening gradually throughout the US Cavalry.

Connie returned to Fargo with Ann to await the birth of their second child. She would find there many other young mothers whose husbands were either in the Pacific or European Theaters. Their lives for the next two years or so would be to provide support systems for one another. James Hardesty Critchfield Jr. was born in Fargo at St.

Luke's Hospital on December 14, 1943. Jim was not to see him until he returned from the war.

Connie with Ann and Jimmy in North Dakota in 1945

Jim, by this time a lieutenant colonel, traveled from San Diego to Norfolk by train and couldn't believe what he found waiting for him there. He was to be the senior officer on board the new fast troop carrier, the *Billy Mitchell*. He found that in addition to his own troops, he was in charge of several hundred prisoners whose charges would be dropped once out to sea. The colonel commanding the embarkation port said, "Colonel, you can put the blame on Eleanor, the president's wife, if you do not like what I have been ordered to do. The prisoners will be marched to your ship two-by-two by white Military Police companies and locked in Hold Number Four. They are then your responsibility." Lieutenant Colonel Critchfield, then twenty-six years old, not only had his men and the prisoners, but also a large number of air force bomber crew replacements, a group of twenty Red Cross girls led by movie star Madeline Carroll, and a small team of US Marines manning whatever defensive weapons the ship carried. Somehow, he managed to maintain discipline aboard ship. As for the prisoners, they were divided up into small groups and assigned to experienced noncoms, who were told to keep them in line.

When they arrived in Casablanca, all but the air force officers were put aboard a French forty and eight troop train with two old coaches and the rest boxcars. They were to cross the Atlas Mountains and arrive at Oran on the Mediterranean coast of Algeria. The family has heard this story, but it is one worth repeating. The Red Cross girls were put in one coach car, and there were strict orders that they be protected. The officers were in the other coach car and the troops were piled into the boxcars. The long trek began. When they arrived at Oujda, high in the Atlas Mountains, the French train official said they would be stopping there until daylight. So Jim allowed everyone to detrain but not to leave the area. Everyone was surprised when about 2:00 a.m., switching engines began moving sections of the train around, and within thirty minutes the reassembled train was again under way. Dawn was just breaking when there was a short rest stop. Sergeant Watkins, the same Sergeant Watkins that helped to train the jazz band from Kansas City, came to inform Jim that not all the troops were onboard. Those missing had apparently gone AWOL into the town of Oujda looking for wine and women, obviously thinking they did not have to be back until dawn. Jim quickly put two of his best officers and several older noncoms on a train going back to Oujda with orders to round up the strays. According to their account, they found the men at the local whorehouse very hung over but not very chastened. Jim, in the meantime, was being chewed out by the commander of the US replacement depot in Oran, who charged, "Colonel, you failed to maintain discipline among your troops." Before he had the book thrown at him, however, two senior cavalry officers intervened, and the episode was declared history.

At Oran, the officers and troops of the Tenth Cavalry were shocked to learn that the Tenth was to be deactivated, its colors returned to the United States, and its personnel disbursed through the replacement depot. Having come right to the edge of the war zone together, the men took it hard. At the final dress parade, three noncommissioned officers who had been with Jim from the beginning—Sergeant Major Stafford and Master Sergeants Watkins and Ellis—each, while standing at attention, saluted and spoke of all that they had experienced together, thanking the colonel for his efforts on their behalf. They were men close to tears. They all knew that so much of the long effort to build a battle-ready black unit was being cast to the winds. Kept together, Jim knew that these splendid soldiers would have performed well any mission given to them. Jim has commented that he emerged from this experience with the deep conviction that full integration within the US armed forces was a national necessity. Yet, it was a poignant moment for all.

In 1992, General Colin Powell, then chief of the Joint Chiefs of Staff, dedicated a monument to the Buffalo Soldier at Fort Leavenworth to honor the troopers of the Ninth and Tenth Cavalries. In response to a letter from Jim telling him the stories related above, General Powell in a letter dated June 16, 1992 said, "The story of the 10th Cavalry is one that we have ignored too long. The Buffalo Soldier Monument is another step towards recognizing the significant achievements of those who served our nation so well, despite the obstacles facing them. Even though the monument portrays a black soldier, the contributions of the white officers who led those soldiers will be remembered as well. You too faced the obstacles erected by a society plagued by racism and bigotry."

In reestablishing contact in 1992 with some of his former noncoms, he learned sadly that Sergeant Watkins was killed in Italy by his own troops and thrown into a canal. "You know," said the writer, "he was a very strict disciplinarian—especially with Black troops." Jim also heard that the prisoners from the *Billy Mitchell* who had been set free went into the Quartermaster Corps and ran a thriving black market business in Italy. But there were also some real success stories. Chief Warrant Officer Gaines, who described himself as one of Jim's dit-da-dit operators, finished the war in Europe and served in Korea, Okinawa, and Germany. After he retired from the army, he went to work for McGraw Hill Publishing and retired as manager of purchasing. After he retired, he became involved in Vision Quest, an organization to teach disadvantaged boys from the Los Angeles ghetto the skills of horsemanship. Sergeant Steele, who described himself as a tall, skinny kid from Harlem, wrote that Jim's confidence in him gave him the impetus he needed at the time. In 1948, he earned a commission as a second lieutenant and retired as a major in 1965, the day before his two sons entered West Point as cadets. One son was the first Black varsity football player at the academy and commanded a company in Vietnam. The other son is a full colonel. Major Steele retired in 1984 from Johnson & Johnson Corporate Headquarters, where he was the director of Administrative Services. Major Steel said to Jim in a letter in 1992, "You would be surprised, Colonel Critchfield, how often your name has come up in Buffalo Soldier conversations as the champion of the cause for which we were all fighting, the opportunity to show that we were as well trained and prepared to defend our country as any soldiers or sailors sent to any part of the world during World War II. It's too bad that we never got a chance to prove that."

THE REAL BATTLE BEGINS

Jim was assigned to the staff of General Lucien K. Truscott, commander of the Sixth Corps in Italy, and spent several months shuttling among the Third, Forty-Fifth and Thirty-Sixth Divisions. Then he was headquartered in Naples, where he spent the next several months working on a task force planning the invasion of southern France. From this point on, it becomes difficult, in this family history, to chronicle events. Why? Well, there are several books written about these events. Not everyone in the family wants to read about these battles in detail nor is there space here to cover them. But for those who wish to read more about the war than is contained here, I strongly recommend that you take advantage of our library. In it, there are three excellent books covering in detail the specific events that Jim took part in during and up to the end of the war. They are:

1. 141st Infantry Regiment Assoc. *Five Years, Five Countries, Five Campaigns: An Account of the 141st Infantry in World War II*. Munich: F. Bruckmann KG, 1945. Jim was one of three officers who put together this book after the war. Most of the sections from the landing in southern France through to the end of the war were written by him.

2. Col. Vincent M. Lockhart. *T-Patch to Victory: The 36th "Texas" Division*. Canyon, TX: Staked Plains Press, 1981. Vince Lockhart also went on to the CIA after the war; he was with the 142nd Regiment and for a period was the division historian.

3. *The United States Seventh Army, Report of Operations France and Germany, 1944–45*, three volumes. Heidelberg, Germany: Aloys Graef, 1946.

From these published works, I will extract stories of the major events of the war, as Jim experienced them. I might also add that Jim's extensive WW II records, uniforms, and photos were donated to the National WWII Museum in New Orleans in 2015 and are available there for any interested parties.

First, there was the landing in France on August 15, 1944. What so often happens to people who propose planned strategies happened to Jim. He was given the task to carry out the invasion plan he worked on. The Seventh Army's Sixth Corps, under the command of General Truscott, landed three divisions on the shores of southern France in the area of the famed Riviera. Jim was commander of the Second Battalion of the 141st Infantry of the Thirty-Sixth Division. To give a sense of the emotion of the moment, the message from General Patch, Seventh Army commander, read over the ship's loudspeakers on the evening of August 14 is repeated here:

> We are embarking for a decisive campaign in Europe. Side by side, wearing the same uniform and using the same equipment, battle experienced French and American soldiers are fighting with a single purpose and common aim—destruction of Nazism and the German Army. The agonized people of Europe anxiously await our coming. We cannot and will not fail. We will not stop until the last vestige of German tyranny has been completely crushed. No greater honor could come to us than this opportunity to fight to the bitter end in order to restore all that is good and decent and righteous in mankind. We are an inspired Army. God be with us.

Jim says that not only emotions but tensions were high that night aboard ship. He for one could not sleep and spent the hours awaiting dawn reading Edna Ferber's *A Peculiar Treasure*, something he had picked up somewhere. It was the first time he had ever read about Jewish family life in the Midwest, and he became so absorbed in the story that he stayed up all night to finish it. By 0505 hours, the troops had finished the traditional "last breakfast" of steak and eggs, loaded into the navy landing craft, and prepared to hit the beach. The Second Battalion landed on the rocky beach west of Cap Drammont. By midnight of D-Day, the beach had been taken and they were twelve miles inland getting ready to cut the main highway from Cannes to Frejus. Viva La France! Vive L'Amerique!

From August until after Christmas 1944, as the German forces retreated up the Rhone River valley, Jim led his Second Battalion into the Roubian Valley of Montelimar through the Vosge Mountains into the vineyards of Alsace. During this four-month period, his battalion losses from killed or wounded in action were four times its average strength. Although the fighting in the Vosges Mountains described by Jim in a letter later to Aunt Helen in Iowa as "heavily wooded, cold, rainy, snowy and thoroughly miserable" was the longest action they endured, living in foxholes for 132 days, it was the battle for Montelimar in the Roubian valley in late August, a week after the landing in southern France, that was so dramatic and caused a great deal of tension between Jim and his division commander, Major General John Dahlquist. Dahlquist had ordered Jim to take his battalion across the Roubian Valley into Montelimar and capture the town, interdicting main German military traffic on the north-south highway, which was critical to the Germans. Although they actually reached and cut the highway, the battalion suffered tremendous losses and finally after repeated attacks was ordered to withdraw because of heavy German tank fire. They had been fighting for almost thirty-two straight hours. By the end of the fighting, they had lost all their equipment except for a tank destroyer and a truck. They carried their wounded in the truck and withdrew to the command post, where Jim found the 141st regimental commander, Colonel Harmony, wounded. He placed Jim in command of the regiment. The next day, Generals Dahlquist and Stack, the Thirty-Sixth Division deputy, arrived in the area, and a very bitter then acting Regimental Commander Critchfield called the whole Montelimar operation a tactical error and an unmitigated disaster. For months after that, Jim would not speak to Dalhquist, except for the required "Yes, sir and No, sir." Many years later, General Lucian Truscott, commander of the VI Corps, told Jim he had been astonished to learn that the Thirty-Sixth had sent a single isolated battalion out into the open plains of the Roubian to attack Montelimar instead of sticking to the high ground. In fact, Truscott had flown into the area just after that to inform Dahlquist he was relieved of duty but later agreed to leave him in command. These were the real tribulations of battle.

It was after this action that Jim received his first Bronze Star. The citation read, "While deployed around the crest of a hill, the 2nd Battalion was completely cut off from all friendly units. The ammunition supply was exhausted and enemy tanks and infantrymen were closing in from four sides. Lieutenant Colonel Critchfield gave the order to withdraw immediately after dark. The battalion command post was set ablaze; 40 casualties remained to be evacuated and only two jeeps were available; confusion threatened the battalion. But Lieutenant Colonel Critchfield, working in the face of heavy fire, calmed his troops so effectively, he converted a near rout into a successful withdrawal." I venture to say that General Dahlquist did not write this citation.

Back with his Second Battalion, Jim and his men proceeded after the Germans who had withdrawn into the dense woods of the Vosge Mountains. Twice during those three months, his men fought for a period of thirty-one days, twenty-four hours a day, without being relieved. Early in December, they came out of the Vosges at Kayserberg in Alsace, where for three weeks they faced the first German offensive. Jim said that it was a strange, naked feeling to look out across the open Alsace plain after months of nothing but high-forested mountains. The panoramic view of the level, vine-covered land stretching for miles around gave them a feeling of exposure that made them uneasy—like strangers arriving in a foreign land. They marched to the little town of Riquewihr. For almost a week of continuous fighting, they succeeded in capturing the area and checking efforts of the German Nineteenth Army to destroy the Thirty-Sixth Division's positions. For their actions and bravery there, they received the Presidential Unit Citation, the highest award that is made to a military unit. And Jim during the time received the Silver Star.

The citation for the Silver Star reads:

> When approximately 700 Germans officer candidates infiltrated through friendly lines and launched an assault which threatened to overrun the battalion command post, Lt. Col. Critchfield swiftly deployed his headquarters personnel. Then moving through heavy small arms fire to an exposed position in a town, he fired into the midst of the Germans with a rifle and machine gun. Though bullets chipped the wall, he remained in his position and directed artillery and mortar fire. The enemy began to withdraw.
>
> Then, braving a heavy enemy artillery barrage, he led two tank destroyers to a position where fire could be delivered upon the retreating Germans, and standing on the exposed deck of one tank destroyer, directed fire until the enemy was completed routed.

This action took place on December 12, 1944. The town was Riquewihr, today a charming medieval village with a stone tower guarding its entrance. An army friend some years ago gave a poster of this village to Jim. You can visualize what hand-to-hand combat might have been like there in the fourteenth century and again during the twentieth century. This land had been a battleground for many centuries.

Just before Christmas, Jim and his men were pulled out of the Colmar sector and billeted in a suburb of Strasbourg. Strasbourg, the beautiful cathedral city of Alsace, seemed heaven-sent for these weary soldiers, and they remember it as the most wonderful Christmas. But in January, after his orders to remove to a rest camp were canceled, his unit was alerted that the Germans were on an offensive. Everything was covered with ice and snow; morale was low and the whole outlook quite gloomy. Nevertheless, they once and for all ended the offensive ideas of the Germans in that area. For January and February 1945, the battalion spent most of its time north of Strasbourg, and it was a relatively quiet period. But on March 15, the entire front blazed into action, and Jim's battalion drove north to the Siegfried Line and on through to the Rhine River in Germany. It was at the Siegfried Line that Jim received a hit, a flesh wound in the back from an artillery shell. In over 220 days of fighting that was the only time he was ever hit.

When they reached the Rhine River, Jim was given ten days at a rest hotel in Cannes, the area where he had landed those many months before. He lived in the lap of luxury. He then returned to the real world in early April and joined his battalion at Mannheim. They pushed off into the heart of southern Germany in the last drive of the war. They drove down into the heart of the Bavarian redoubt of Nazism through the Bavarian mountain lakes and on into Austria. When the cease-fire order came on May 5, Jim's battalion was fighting a bunch of SS troops inside Austria.

The Germans got the order "Halt in Place," the same as Jim did. The German officer came over to surrender his command. Jim's men were sedate and quiet, and they felt a tired sense of relief that the war in Europe was finally over.

LESSONS LEARNED

It is time to pause and reflect on the impact the WW II experience had on this twenty-eight-year-old young man from North Dakota. It was profound and shaped him for the rest of his life. He frequently commented that his war experience was the most important thing that ever happened to him and the most unforgettable. I only saw Jim cry three times during our thirty years together—twice when his two brothers, Bill and Pat, died, and the third when I came down for breakfast one morning, and he was reading a story in the *Washington Post* about a soldier whose comrades were lost in battle in Europe in 1945. He was more than crying; he was sobbing. It shocked me into silence until he recovered enough to share with me the misery and memories this brought back to him. We never spoke of it again.

But our conversations over the years and the travels we made to various battlefields left no doubt in my mind that WW II was the defining moment in Jim's life. I have tried to sum it up with the following observations.

> While extensive training from 1939–44 prepared him for battle, he was at the same time awed by the increasing responsibilities put before him at such a young age. Battlefield casualties thrust him rapidly into positions of command, ones he had not sought or imagined. He became a leader.

The men he fought and lived with in foxholes from August 1944 to May 1945 became his friends for life. Even though not Catholic, Father Fenton, who traveled with the battalion, became a lifelong spiritual adviser. He revered Father Fenton and emulated him when he could. Many years later, Jim let his thoughts about religion be known in a condolence letter he wrote to his aunt Helen about the death of her son at an early age. He said, "It was during the war when I first began to understand and accept that only in the history and teaching of Christianity was I able to survive great personal sorrows and losses."

Decisions he had to make in the heat of battle equipped him for the many decisions he had to make in supporting US policy during the Cold War when he joined the newly created CIA and immediately became a senior division chief.

The horrors of war, in particular the dropping of the atomic bomb on Hiroshima and Nagasaki, always reminded him during critical decision-making times to press for peace.

But he also saw the need for humor and a time for lightheartedness during those most serious of times. He loved to tell the story of sharing his villa with Ingrid Bergman or relating his predicament when his enlisted men went AWOL in Algeria and were found the next morning at the local brothel. The stories allowed him to maintain his sanity.

Lieutenant James H
Critchfield prewar

Colonel James H.
Critchfield postwar

AFTER THE WAR AND BEFORE THE CIA

Just after VE Day, Jim was put in charge temporarily of the
141st Regiment, which was located in Ulm in south central
Germany. As part of the recreation program, the regiment
had organized a summer theater in Ulm. One of several
productions staged during the summer was *Our Town* with
Raymond Massey playing the lead. But the highlight of
that time in Ulm was when he turned his living quarters
over to actress Ingrid Bergman. One day a jeep arrived at
the command post and a man jumped out and introduced
himself. "I'm Benny," he said. It was Jack Benny, Ingrid
Bergman, and a troupe of entertainers. No one had let them
know in Ulm that they were planning a stop there. Jim
graciously gave Miss Bergman his quarters, and, as the
story goes, when he escorted her there, she said, "Stay and
talk with me." They sat on the balcony, and Miss Bergman,

while brushing her hair, talked and talked. It was one of those unforgettable moments in life.

After the excitement of the Bergman encounter, Jim found himself hospitalized and after two weeks or so of tests, the army decided it was combat fatigue and released him to return to the United States. He arrived on the East Coast by ship and flew to Fargo to be reunited with Connie, Ann, Jimmy, Mother, and siblings. It was the first time he had seen son Jimmy, who was almost three years old. This was when Jimmy made the famous statement, "He's got legs." Jimmy, having only known Jim as the man in the famous family portrait, thought that is what Daddy looked like—a man with no legs. That reunion only lasted forty-eight hours before Jim had to leave for New York. That was the difference between regular army and volunteer army. Those who joined up or were drafted to fight in World War II were now back with their families picking up where they left off. The regulars, however, did not have the luxury of long holidays.

The Germans were now defeated, and the question of how to deal with Germany in postwar Europe would be the next challenge. With soldiering over, the army hand-selected a number of officers to attend graduate schools in the United States to broaden their focuses. The world of politics now commanded center stage. Jim entered Columbia University in September 1946 taking a cram course in geopolitics put together for officers that would face assignments in Europe.

After the Columbia experience, Jim returned to Germany and in May 1946 became head of the counterintelligence branch of G-2 in Bad Tolz under General Truscott, who was then in command of the Third Army, which by then had become the occupation force. That was Jim's first experience in intelligence. His group soon moved to Heidelberg. Counterintelligence and security were all wrapped up together in Jim's duties. He felt as if he had a million duties. Some of them were: civil and military security in the zone, controlling travel across Germany's border under US control, supporting the war crimes trials, responsibility for security within the POW camps, and setting up civilian internment camps. The Americans had arrested and interned several hundred thousand Germans who had been officials of the Nazi Party but, once arrested, had not addressed the disposal of these people. They were not accused of any acts other than being members of the Nazi Party. It was much more difficult to handle the individual cases than it had been to arrest them. Eventually, the problem was turned over to German authorities, who established a court system to review the cases.

An example of a type of operation G-2 became involved in during that early postwar period was "Operation Grab Bag." It was a 1940s version of the Saigon boat people or, even closer to our shores, the Haitian boat escapees. The boat action in 1946 was on the Danube River. Right after the war, many people from Eastern Europe, fearing the Russians, fled westward on foot and by boat. A large number of these were from royal families in the nations being communized under Soviet control. These displaced persons boarded boats and proceeded up the Danube in a prolonged flight followed by advancing Soviet forces. The boats went as far as they could into Germany and when out of danger docked, and most of the passengers remained and lived on board until they could sort out their lives. Not surprising in a population like that, the boats became a community unto their own and soon black marketeering in both guns and goods brought these people to the attention of the US Army military and security forces in Germany. "Operation Grab Bag," under the command of Lieutenant Colonel Critchfield, was organized to get this group under control. Early one morning, Jim and his team raided the boats on the Danube and confiscated all weapons and black market goods. An orderly census was taken of those living onboard, except for one American colonel who was taken by surprise that morning. He had been "staying over" with his Hungarian countess. Eventually, of course, those displaced persons found their way into society and out of reach of the Soviets. This operation had been impressive enough for the new Third Army commander, Lieutenant General Geoffrey Keyes, to send a letter of appreciation and commendation to Jim for his "outstanding performance of duty during the recent operation on the Danube River."

Connie and the children arrived in Heidelberg in August 1946 with a new Mercury station wagon, which saw fifteen thousand miles of French, German, and Austrian roads in six months. Shortly after that, General Keyes was appointed commanding general US Forces Austria, replacing Mark Clark, and he asked that Jim be reassigned as chief of the G-2 counterintelligence and an added responsibility for positive intelligence operations. After a short delay to find housing, the family in March 1947 joined him in Vienna. This was a good time for dependents in Germany and Austria. They were able to travel around the beautiful countryside, over to Paris, down to Italy, and soak up all the culture of a Europe that, though war-torn, was still a magnificent place. At that time, Vienna was a city of intrigue, epitomized in the movie *The Third Man*. Vienna was under Four Power control and was more or less in the center of the Soviet Zone of Occupation. The four powers, which were constantly testing one another, ran in what today's world would be looked at as quite primitive operations. The main US target now was the whole scope of Soviet activities in Austria. It was a lively time.

In addition to counterintelligence activities, Jim was responsible for analyzing and reporting to General Keyes and to Washington on the strategic and economic situation in postwar Austria. Working closely with Jim was Henry Pleasants, a journalist from Philadelphia, who was the chief US political liaison officer to the Austrian chancellor. Jim and Henry would remain close friends for life. Together, they produced the required weekly economic and political report on the local situation. In the course of this assignment, he worked closely with Eleanor Dulles, sister of John Foster and Allen Dulles, the Wall Street lawyers who were to figure prominently in the Washington scene in the 1950s. Eleanor was then the head of the Economic Section of the American Legation in Vienna.

Despite efforts to extend his tour through 1948, the Pentagon informed Jim he would be reassigned in early 1948. He knew not where. He really had no idea at the time what the future would hold for him. In a letter to his close wartime friend Park Hough, he said that his choices would be (1) an assignment to the Armed Forces Staff College, (2) a two-year course at Yale on international affairs, and (3) associating in some capacity with the CIA. During his tours in Heidelberg and Vienna, Jim had met several officers from the newly formed Central Intelligence Agency, among them Richard Helms, a future CIA director. He liked what he saw.

Two letters preceded Jim to the United States. One was from Colonel Bixel, director of intelligence of the US Forces in Austria, and one was from Eleanor Dulles. Colonel Bixel wrote to the director of intelligence of the US Army General Staff stating that Jim had done a magnificent job, and Bixel considered him to be especially qualified in intelligence procedures and techniques and thoroughly grounded on the situation in Austria. Eleanor Dulles wrote her brother John Foster in New York and urged Foster to meet Jim. She said that Jim had been working on some of the most strategically important policy matters and had contributed in notable fashion to the work. She felt that it would be extremely important that he continue, if not in the army, at least in work that deals with such matters. She felt that since many people were not quick enough to see the significance of events, it was always gratifying to be associated with those who did. She felt strongly that Jim would contribute further in the future to the aims and programs in which Foster and she had such great interest. With such a letter, it comes as no surprise to learn that when Jim visited Foster Dulles in New York, he called in his brother Allen to meet him.

The decision to leave the army and join the newly created Central Intelligence Agency was not easy. While his future in the army was being decided, he took a course in advanced armor at Fort Knox. After Armored School, he was assigned to the Operations Division of the US Army General Staff and was selected to be one of six officers to attend Princeton University for three years to obtain a PhD. The Bixel letter no doubt played a part in bringing Jim to the General Staff's attention. The Dulles letter also brought Jim to the attention of the CIA. But by mid-1948, Jim had decided on the CIA route. There was a lot of pressure on him to remain in the army, where he was known to have a future. Even to this day, people who knew him then and know him now say this. Park Hough, for example, in a Christmas 1993 letter said, "I don't know how many times during my 33 years in the Army and since, I have said to so many that you were the finest Army officer with whom I had ever served and that unquestionably had you chosen the Army for a career, you would have risen to Chairman of the Joint Chiefs of Staff."

No one can ever say with certainty why he decides to walk down one road instead of another. This was 1948. The army in 1948 was a very different one from the army Jim had joined in 1939. The single most important event to change this was the dropping of the first atomic bomb on Hiroshima in 1945. This had a revolutionary impact on the science of war and on Jim's approach to a military career. Even if participants refrained from using atomic weapons, which in Jim's view was unlikely, another global war would be infinitely more destructive of civilization than World War II. No nation could possibly win the next war. A superiority of one nation over the other in armament might make it less the loser but hardly the victor. While it would be essential to maintain a well-trained defense establishment, it should only be used as a last resort to ensure that the United States was not militarily defeated in a war of annihilation. Because of the existence of atomic weapons, Jim believed that military solutions to problems had become a negative approach and no longer offered a solution to the economic and sociological problems that beset the world. Because of these deep feelings, he thought that the new CIA would become tremendously vital to the establishment of a politically mature and internationally minded United States capable of assuming the overwhelming responsibility that had been abruptly thrust upon it by the emergence of a strong Soviet Union, whose backing of world communism would provide the challenges for the coming decades. Many years later, he expressed his feelings this way to a close friend. "I began to ask myself whether intelligence in this unsettled world might not assume a new importance in serving the national security needs perhaps equal to the American armed forces."

It was with these thoughts in mind that he said yes to a career with the CIA, and in June 1948 began training to return to Germany to establish a Soviet Operations Base to be headquartered in Munich. In the meantime, Connie was back in Fargo packing up for the new assignment. The plan was that Jim's mother would take Ann and Jimmy to New York by train. Connie and sister Peggy's fiancé, David Baldwin, would drive the car to New York to put it on the ship. All thoughts were on the future. When Jim received the call on June 11 from a state trooper that Connie and David were killed in a collision with a truck near Mechanicsville, Iowa, his world came to an abrupt halt. The state of shock one experiences at times like that took over, and everything seemed to go in reverse. Everyone went back to Fargo, and in the ensuing days after the funerals, Jim worried over what to do. He was without a wife and the children without a mother. Jim felt that it would probably be best for all if he gave up the CIA, returned to Fargo, and established a life of some sort there—that is, stay where your roots were. Jim's mother clearly had put her thinking cap on and, I suspect Jim would agree, solved the family's problem for them. Her advice was that Jim should proceed with his assignment in Germany; she would close up the house in Fargo, and she and Peggy would accompany Jim and the children to Europe. Betty was married by then; Bill was at the University of California, and Pat, age seventeen, would move to Seattle and begin university there. Jim's siblings more or less agree that their mother's practical approach to Jim's future had traces of her own desire for adventure. And who could blame her. Life in Fargo had not been easy, and the prospect of going to Germany provided her with an opportunity to expand her horizons.

THE CIA EXPERIENCE IN GERMANY[2]

The family settled into a house in Harlaching, a suburb community south of Munich, and Jim began his assignment as chief of the Soviet Operations Branch.

He had barely settled in when headquarters ordered him to make an investigation of a German intelligence organization, which had been developed under US Army command immediately after the defeat of Germany in 1945. It had become somewhat of a hot potato, and the old OSS, now CIA officers, had avoided getting involved. As a latecomer to the CIA and the fact he was already in Munich, Jim was tapped to do the work "in addition to his other duties." He commuted back and forth between Munich and Pullach, a village on the Isar River that had become the headquarters of the German organization. What the army had assembled there was much of the surviving intelligence talent of the German Foreign Armies East, complete with their files from four years of wartime operation on the Russian front. The head and driving force in this effort was General Reinhard Gehlen, the wartime head of Foreign Armies East until he was sacked for "defeatism" by order of Hitler in early 1945.

After three months of investigation, Jim informed Washington that what he found at Pullach was a de facto German intelligence service complete with officers and files on Soviet order of battle, but that without working with this group for some time, the CIA could not make a meaningful assessment of its potential to become a factor in German intelligence and the inevitable emergence of West Germany in the Western Alliance. In January 1949, Washington responded that it accepted Jim's recommendations and put him in charge of carrying them out. If Jim had second thoughts about getting involved at Pullach, he graciously put them aside and for the next eight years lived side by side with General Gehlen, through good times and bad, resulting in 1956 in the recognition by the German government of Gehlen's organization as the official West German Intelligence Service known as the Bundesnachrichtendiens (BND). Now, sixty-two years later, the BND is still headquartered at Pullach. For many years, key officers maintained close touch with Jim and treated him with great respect. We were invited there on numerous occasions, and each time, he was toasted as the key figure in allowing the BND to mature and become accepted as Germany's CIA.[3]

Jim's mother more or less took over as his hostess in Munich and, much as she was accustomed to doing in Fargo, socialized with his friends and kept the household running. Life in the postwar fifties was extremely social, and Jim made many new friends among the Americans and the Germans. They remained friends for life. Because of the secretive nature of their jobs, the Americans assigned to Pullach and the Germans became close. They all had two names—a pseudonym used at work and their real names used at home. Their children went to school together. Daughter Ann has remarked that she thought all children had two names. It did not seem strange to them.

On June 17, 1950, Jim married Louise Mithoff, a shy, pretty girl from Lancaster, Ohio, who, with her sister Virginia, had joined the CIA in pursuit of adventure. Both had been in the OSS during the war. The CIA had attracted many talented young men and women who were intrigued by what the postwar world held for them. The "OSSers" were the first group to come. Many were to spend the next thirty years or so in the agency. Louise and Jim's circle of friends, as noted above, came from within their work group. They were great party people. Tom and Peggy Lucid were crowned as the host and hostess with the mostest. They gave wonderful parties. Eberhard and Putchen Blum, Heinz and Christa Herre, Connie and Astrid Kuehlein among the Germans, and Bob and Betty Feldman, Hank and Mary Schardt, Ed and Melba Petty, Jean Pinney and his future wife Pat, Henry and Ginny Pleasants, Bill and Rosemary Graver among the Americans, were and remained good friends of both Jim and Louise. Both Betsy and Tom were born in Germany—Betsy on July 30, 1953, and Tom on December 22, 1955. Family life was good. There were skiing trips in the winter in the nearby German and Swiss Alps, boating in the summer on Lake Starnberg near Pullach, mountain climbing in the spring and fall, and various exploration trips around Europe. Chopin concerts in Salzburg and Wagner festivals in Bayreuth provided culture, rounding out a pleasant life.

The men also managed "to get away from it all" from time to time. Here is a photo probably taken some time in the 1950s in Germany, but we know neither the location nor the occasion. This is one of the family's favorite photographs. It is a "Gotcha" moment.

Men's Night Out

Jim was not a smoker nor did he play poker in later life, but he did enjoy convivial gatherings, particularly when there were bottles on the table.

Surprisingly, though, from 1948 until 1956, Jim and Louise took only one home leave trip. That was in 1951, and it was combined with escorting General Gehlen around the United States. This emphasizes the total absorption Jim gave to the BND assignment. His book clearly outlines the struggles he had with Gehlen, with getting the Gehlen Organization, as the BND was called, accepted, and with ensuring that it found its proper fit in the new Germany under Chancellor Conrad Adenauer. Finally, on March 31, 1956, Jim, standing at the window of his office in the Pullach compound, the office that had once been Martin Bormann's bedroom, watched the American and German flags come down, as they had done for the past eight years. Adenauer had declared the BND the official German intelligence service, and the next day, it would be only the

German flag flying its colors there. In looking back on this event, Jim once remarked that he found it strange that there was no ceremony or even recognition of this historic day—not even a toast of Henkel champagne. He alone witnessed the flag ritual and then crossed the cobblestone courtyard and drove home.

The family was prepared to leave shortly after that for the United States, where Jim would become first deputy chief and then chief of the Eastern European Division. But then tragedy struck once again. Jimmy, age thirteen, off on a Boy Scout outing on the Isar River near Pullach, was accidentally shot in the eye with a pellet gun. Paul Schardt had, unbeknownst to his family or the scoutmaster, brought the gun to the outing, and a friend was playing with it. Jimmy was hiding behind a tree, and the boy shouted, "Don't come out, or I'll shoot." Jimmy peeked around the tree and was hit. It was devastating for Jimmy, and for Jim and the family. Jimmy lost his eye and had to learn how to deal with both the psychological and physical impact of this loss. One never forgets such happenings, but slowly, slowly, one learns to deal with them.

BACK HOME AND IN CHARGE OF EASTERN EUROPEAN AFFAIRS

About six weeks later, as soon as Jimmy was able to travel, the family returned to the States. Jim and Louise purchased Bannockburn, a Civil War era home in Oakton, which was protected by fields on all sides. Its antebellum architecture surrounded by huge boxwoods gave it the aura of southern gentility. It was one of the last holdouts in suburban Fairfax but eventually was swallowed up by townhouse developments. There is no trace of it remaining save for one old elm tree, which can be seen from Route 66. Brother Bill Critchfield remarked once that Bannockburn reminded him of Chekhov's play *The Cherry Orchard*, where an aristocratic family, in financial need, resisted advice from a hardened businessman to cut down the cherry trees to build and sell houses. As the play ends, the saddened family, having lost the home and preparing to leave, hears the sounds of the axes felling the first group of cherry trees.

But the family doted on Bannockburn as long as it lasted. The children settled into an American way of life. After many years, Jim was able to have horses again, and when he was not trimming, mowing, or repairing around the property, he was in the barn taking care of his horses. He introduced daughter Betsy to horses at Bannockburn, and she was hooked for life. Tommy preferred soccer to horses, but he did like to work with his dad around the barn. Jimmy and Ann, in their early teens, went first to public school in Oakton, and then Ann went to Fairfax High School and Jimmy to Flint Hill, a small private school nearby. When they reached school age, Betsy and Tommy also attended Flint Hill. It was typical Americana—no more pseudonyms and no more German English.

Jim in the meantime took on more responsibility at headquarters. He had only been at work a day or so when the revolution in Poland happened. Then the Hungarian Revolution broke out, and by that time he had taken over as chief of the Eastern European Division. In carrying out this job, he shuttled back and forth between CIA Director Allen Dulles and John Foster Dulles, the secretary of state, presenting options of what should be done about Hungary. One day, he was about to brief the Dulles brothers on a detailed plan he had drawn up on Hungary when Undersecretary of State Robert Murphy broke in with the news that Britain and France had landed in Suez. Jim's plan and the Hungarian Revolution were put on the back burner, a bitter pill for many. We all know, of course, that the Soviets won that round in Eastern Europe, and it would be more than thirty years before they were to withdraw.

During the next years, the Soviets solidified their position in Eastern Europe and were expanding their influence in the Middle East and Africa. Soviets such as Khrushchev and Bulganin were talking tough. The KGB was exceedingly effective in propaganda operations, technical penetrations of Western embassies, and use of recruited Western intelligence officers, that is, Philby, McLean, and Burgess. As chief of Eastern Europe, Jim concentrated on developing and training young officers to open stations in all the Eastern European capitals. There was a heavy emphasis on language training and learning the skills of clandestine operations.

Many of these operational cases are still in secret files, but, after the passage of time, some of them have come out. An interesting one involved a Polish intelligence officer, Michael Goleniewski, who for more than three years had sent out to the CIA reports on Polish and Soviet intelligence operations. But suddenly one day he was given a new task, searching for a Polish intelligence officer who was dealing with the West. He knew then that his days were numbered and sent a message that he wanted to come out. He had extensive rolls of microfilm to unload and had selected a dead drop site in a lot with many dead tree stumps. The CIA Warsaw Station chief photographed the spot, and headquarters built a tree stump to look like the rest, but this one had a cache for the film. Goleniewski successfully deposited the film; the CIA man retrieved it, and Goleniewski, bringing his mistress rather than his wife, fled to West Berlin. It turns out that Goleniewski had also been working for the KGB, but in the end, he fled to the West.

This is only one example of many such cases. As chief of an area operational division, Jim actually wore two hats. He gave the final approval for operations run in the field against Soviet and Eastern European targets. He also dealt with the Washington community on policy matters. During the late 1950s, it was the Dulles family that dominated foreign affairs, and Jim was frequently called upon to participate in such matters.

During this time, the flow of talent leaving Eastern Europe for the West was overwhelming. Most of them came via Berlin. Finally, the Soviets put a stop to it by building the Berlin Wall and virtually stopped all traffic to the West. They were also busy in building strong positions in the Middle East and Africa. Because of this, Allen Dulles asked Jim in 1960 if he would take over the Near East Division. Jim protested that he had no experience in the Arab world or the South Asian continent. Mr. Dulles did not care about that; it was the Soviets he wanted Jim to go after. Of course, Jim accepted.

INTRODUCTION TO THE MIDDLE EAST

The mysterious Middle East! For years, the CIA Near East Division had been run by an old boy network that had been left undisturbed to deal with kings and princes. They did not like it at all when this ex-army colonel arrived on the scene to take over. Nor did they have in their RMD (Related Mission Directive—the formal name for their marching orders) instructions to develop operations against the Soviets. Theirs was a territory that dealt with efforts by local opposition parties to overthrow the governments in power, most of which were supported by the United States and some of which had been put into power by the CIA, such as the shah of Iran. It was the era of coup d'états.

When he started traveling to the various stations in the Middle East, he found a lot of talented officers. Soon he gained their confidence. He recalls that on his first visit to Beirut, he had lunch with three of the most senior case officers—Jack O'Connell, Jim Burke, and Duane Rames. In making conversation, he asked them where they were from. "South Dakota," said Jack. "North Dakota," said Jim. "South Dakota," said Duane. Jim was nonplussed. Not everyone was Eastern Establishment after all!

As with the Eastern European Division, he quickly developed a language program and sent as many young case officers as he could to a total immersion one-year Arabic course in Beirut. His son-in-law, Dan Webster, was among this group. Most of these officers went on to important field assignments, and many of them in later years held senior positions in the agency, including Dan.

Heads of state in the Middle East for the most part continued to be replaced by coup d'états. Syria was one of the most dramatic examples of that. In the early 1960s, some twelve to thirteen coups overthrew governments there. The NE Division could point with pride that it had advance intelligence from penetrations of these opposition groups on all of these coups, save one. The one it did not know about was staged out of Beirut by an opposition party, the PPS, a party supported by the CIA. When the leaders staged the coup on New Year's Eve, however, they had sent all of the known CIA agents on missions to Europe and South America. So, embarrassingly, the agency did not know of the attempt until it happened. It was a type of sweet revenge when this coup failed.

During the early 1960s, the Soviets became very active in Egypt. They got into central Africa, Léopoldville, and Stanleyville, operating mainly through Cairo. Egypt's President Gamal Abd el Nasser was the key instrument of the Soviets during the 1960s, but he in turn also embroiled them in conflicts in which they would have preferred not getting involved.

There has never been a quiet period in the Middle East, and the decade of the 1960s was no exception. First, Egyptian President Nasser's dream, the United Arab Republic, broke up in 1961. Then in 1962 the Yemen War broke out, a war which was actually an outgrowth of anticolonialist pressures on the British but which all too soon involved the Soviets directly. The Soviets went into this conflict reluctantly, but they had little choice, because the weapons of war Cairo was using had come from them. They were even forced to put Soviet pilots behind the controls of the TU-16 medium bombers, because the Egyptians simply didn't have the skills to use them effectively. The US State Department did not want to get involved, but there were certain covert actions that took place to thwart Egyptian-Soviet advances in Yemen. The building of the Soviet presence in the Middle East both from the Egyptian-Red Sea-Yemen flank and from the Iraq-Syrian flank on the other side of the Arabian Peninsula together with the escalating Arab-Israeli conflict produced a wild ride for Western intelligence operatives in the area. There was never a lack of things on which to report. The CIA Near East Division was right in the thick of it.

As if that were not enough to deal with, in the middle of all this, the Chinese attacked India. Jim was in Beirut when this happened, planning to join his local chief Arthur Callahan's family for Thanksgiving dinner. He received an urgent message from Dick Helms to proceed immediately to New Delhi. The Averell Harriman mission was leaving Washington for India, and Helms wanted Jim to get there posthaste to deal with the Indian government on intelligence issues. Jim remembers that before he left the city for the Beirut airport, he stopped at Sheikh & Sons Restaurant, which had a big sign in the window— "Thanksgivin dinner complete with all the trimmins and grandberries." So he had his turkey after all. When he reported to the embassy in New Delhi the next day, as he was going up the steps, who did he run into coming down those steps but brother Richard Patrick, "brother Pat." It was reminiscent of the meeting of Livingstone and General Gordon: "Dr. Livingstone, I presume." Brother Pat was then a freelance journalist reporting on the region.

The China conflict coupled with the Indo-Pak War and the Kashmir conflict resulted in Jim returning many times to India. But he didn't stop there; one had to be evenhanded when dealing in this part of the world. Pakistan too had to be dealt with. The major interest there for the United States, as far as intelligence was concerned, was to make both India and Pakistan aware that there was something bigger than their personal conflict and, therefore, the CIA worked with both sides to develop systems for dealing with the Communist Chinese threat. For these reasons, Jim also made several trips to Pakistan.

This was the time that brother Pat was in India teaching at Naghpur University and stirring up his own little conflicts. With the tremendous energy that his youth and never-ending curiosity produced, his activities soon came to the attention of the Indian intelligence service. Jim had earlier assured Malek, the chief of intelligence, that his younger brother was only what he appeared to be, an inquiring journalist somewhat prone to being impetuous. He hoped that if he got into trouble, Malek would alert his men to watch out for him. Well, it wasn't long before that need arose. On a tip from the Delhi Chief of Station David Blee, Pat flew off to Kashmir to investigate the report of the theft of the Prophet's hair, an incident that aroused the "Lion of Kashmir" Abdullah to revolt against the Indian government. Pat turned out to be the only Western journalist in Kashmir on that occasion. He obviously came to the attention of Indian security and soon found himself being gently hustled back to New Delhi and out of India. But not before he got his scoop and reported in detail on the Prophet's hair and on the riots in Kashmir.

Meanwhile, back in the Arab Middle East, the 1967 Arab-Israeli War occurred, slowing down Soviet activities there. The Yemen War ended, and for the latter half of the 1960s, two major activities were taking place. Jim and the NE Division were in the middle of both. First, very secret talks were going on between King Hussein and the Israelis aimed at settling their specific bilateral problems. (These, of course, are no longer "secrets.") It took many years, but these talks eventually culminated in a Jordanian-Israeli rapprochement. Second, through their intelligence counterparts in Iran, Saudi Arabia, and Egypt, the CIA developed a counterweight against the Soviet use of their satellites—Syria, Iraq, Algeria, and Sudan—by bringing together the shah of Iran, King Feisal of Saudi Arabia, and eventually Anwar Sadat of Egypt to diminish Soviet influence in the area. Sadat's throwing out of the Soviets from Egypt was a big blow not only to Soviet presence in the Middle East but also to its prestige there.

In looking back on his eight years as division chief, Jim could point with some personal pride to the number of Arabic-speaking case officers in the Near East stations who were running effective and valuable operations against hostile, extremist groups there; he could take some credit for influencing the heads of state of the moderate Arab nations to become more aggressive against Soviet encroachments in their area, and he could, in India, claim success in bringing the Indian intelligence service up to speed on dealing with the Chinese Communist threat.

ON TO OIL, WATER, FOOD GRAINS, AND FERTILIZERS?

As exciting as life was in NE Division, there came a time when Jim felt that he wanted to turn his job over to someone else. But he was not prepared to go back to Europe. The Middle East bug had bitten.

You cannot deal with the Middle East for long without coming to realize the importance of oil. It has always been so. That was why the Western world and the Communist world were vying for positions of influence there. But as long as oil was $5 a barrel, and there seemed to be a limitless supply of it, and the producing governments continued to support Western objectives, the US government and intelligence community did not focus too much attention on the subject of oil as a threat to national security. Let's say that we took it for granted. The United States produced most of its own oil. It only cost twenty-five cents a gallon, so why worry?

But there were rumblings that maybe we should start worrying. The major oil companies, the so-called Seven Sisters, took note of the formation of OPEC, established in Venezuela in 1968, by the main producing and exporting countries, most of which were in the Middle East and North Africa. There were suggestions that if the producing countries did not get more money for their oil, they might expropriate or nationalize the companies.

It was the beginning of an era in which Middle East oil was going to be a central issue on the world agenda. Not only oil, but also water was becoming an issue. The Tigris, Euphrates, and Jordan Rivers, for example, flow through many of the region's nation states, and disputes on the use of the waters were already being heard. These were arid lands remember. Also, the Green Revolution had not yet happened and there was concern that the world population would be competing for food grains and fertilizers to feed their growing numbers. Jim felt that these were critical issues and that the intelligence community should be delving into them more deeply than they were. These subjects—oil, water, food grains, and fertilizers— formed the basis of an operational proposal by Jim to then Director of Central Intelligence Dick Helms to form a group that would treat these as intelligence issues and collect and analyze information from all sources on the OPEC nations, the oil companies, and the consuming nations in Europe, Japan, and the Western Hemisphere. It was his belief that if the US government did not get on top of these issues of critical basic resources worldwide, it was going to be difficult to deal with them when the crises emerged.

DCI Helms agreed and gave Jim the go-ahead to develop his project. It was one that crossed division lines and affected jurisdictional rights. It required a lot of diplomacy to get division chiefs, sometimes called "barons," to allow Jim to deal on their turf. But with the DCI behind you, arms were twisted without too much pain. When Jim left NE Division to organize this project, many people couldn't understand what he was up to. Some thought he was out to pasture. But others knew he was on to something. My boss, for example, William Freeman, who was getting ready to retire, called me in one day and said he had recommended me for a job in Critchfield's project. He said, "It is still a very secret operation and has to do with dealing with oil, water, food ... oh, what the Hell, when he interviews you pretend you know what he is talking about. I know it will be a great job. Critchfield is a forward thinker, one of the few we have." That was my introduction to my new job. I must have pretended well when I was interviewed, because he hired me.

Now, if you are wondering how Jim became an expert on oil, the expertise that led him after retirement to spend another fifteen years as an oil adviser in the Middle East, stay tuned. I can't tell all, but we were definitely not out to pasture. Starting in 1968, a team of officers of all ages began to organize themselves into something resembling a think tank. There were about ten people to begin with. They moved out into the business world contacting American, European, and Middle Eastern businessmen, first to learn from them the business from the bottom up (no, we never actually worked in the oilfields), but we met frequently with these experts and had long sessions with them, learning from them all the intricacies of the price of a barrel of oil and so forth and eventually playing back to them our observations and analyses of what we saw going on in the oil arena. We became experts on OPEC and were the principal collectors of intelligence on OPEC during the early 1970s. We had close contacts in the main oil-producing nations too—Iran, Saudi Arabia, Libya, Bahrain, Kuwait, the UAE, and Oman. The giant American oil companies were anxious to cooperate once they were briefed on the nature of this intelligence venture. And retired officers of these oil firms also joined the effort and made major contributions. Out of this came two types of products, one a monthly newsletter analyzing both the economic and political trends of the OPEC world and of the Western consumers. This was shared with all contacts in the Middle East, Europe, Japan, and the United States and was used by them to bring their influence to bear wherever they could. The other product was the collection and dissemination of intelligence on matters of interest to the CIA, National Security Council, Defense Department and State Department.

During this time, Jim was actually holding down two jobs, but they were so complementary that it was like one big job. In 1973, he was appointed national intelligence officer for energy, a newly created position that was to deal with all government agencies in the production of intelligence estimates on the energy situation. It provided the perfect vehicle for the flow of information from the secret operation to those in the US government who needed to be kept up to speed on the struggle of the oil companies in Libya, in Iran, and in Saudi Arabia who were demanding a major restructuring of their relationships, giving them a larger piece of the action and leading eventually to their control of the world's largest reserves of oil and natural gas. This was dramatic stuff, because the oil producers realized that finally they were dealing from positions of strength. They had the oil, and we needed it. By the time of the first oil shock of 1973 when oil went from $5 a barrel to $13 overnight, this small group of dedicated intelligence officers led by Jim and the equally dedicated people from the business world of energy who were cooperating with us were able to put together fairly sophisticated analyses of the current problems. Some of you remember the gas lines in 1973. Rising prices of gasoline were real. Jim's project was able to contribute substantially to the effort of the US government to understand and formulate policy to deal with the crisis.

Some other interesting events were taking place during this time. The one that was to have a lasting impact on Jim and shape his future for a number of years was the overthrow of the old sultan of Oman by his young son Qaboos. This happened in 1970. This incidentally was not a CIA operation. But there could be no denying that the British had a hand in it. The last holdout of the British was the Persian Gulf. They long had a dominant position there. The Omani Sultan Said treated his citizens like children. There was no electricity, telephones, newspapers, or radios; the walls to the city gates of the capital, Muscat, were closed each day at sundown, and people had to walk around with lanterns. There were no paved roads, a few hospitals, and only boys were allowed in the small number of schools there. It was a feudal, backward country. Most of its bright young men who could get out did. For some reason, the old sultan did send his son Qaboos to Sandhurst Military Academy, and it was there that Qaboos made important British friends who have remained friends to this day. These were the friends who helped him in his decision to overthrow his father. The old man fled to London, where he remained in exile until his death a few years later, and Qaboos, with British assistance, began to build his nation, which today is a masterpiece of modern architecture, economic development, and social awareness.

But Qaboos realized that he could not allow the British to dominate him during those formative years, and very quietly he let it be known he would be happy to meet with select unofficial representatives of the US government to discuss an enhanced role for Americans in

Oman, particularly in the development of business. A small delegation of American VIPs, headed by former Treasury Secretary Robert B. Anderson, slipped in and out of Oman shortly after the sultan took over, and from that time on, the sultan invited selected American experts in as advisers and businessmen to help in the country's development. Before long, key Americans from the official Washington scene also found themselves welcome in Oman. Today US relations with Oman remain good.

During the energy crisis starting in 1970, Jim met frequently with Democratic Senator Henry "Scoop" Jackson, who was head of a Senate committee dealing with resources, including oil. He was also a leading Senate figure dealing with relations with the Soviet Union. By 1971, Jim was providing him with copies of our reports produced by the project, and conversations intensified.

After the election of Nixon for the second term, Scoop Jackson prepared a letter to the president proposing the development of a bipartisan energy policy. Just a few days after the inauguration, the president invited Jackson to lunch and discussed the Jackson letter. The exchange moved more rapidly than the senator had anticipated, and they quickly agreed that the scope of the policy had to include Soviet interests in the Middle East, energy per se, and the complex Middle East situation—that is, the Arab-Israeli problems. The president observed that it would be difficult to find a staff chief familiar with all three of these problems. Jackson replied that he knew someone and gave the president Jim Critchfield's name and background. The president wrote down Jim's name, which he later gave to John Ehrlichman with a note to call the CIA and get Critchfield over to the White House. When Jim received the call, he stalled and discussed it with Helms, who by then was preparing to turn over the DCI job and to become the US ambassador to Iran. He urged Jim to take the White House offer and pursue it while continuing his NIO role and the project. Jim reported to Ehrlichman and agreed on terms of reference with some discussion with Hal Saunders and Brent Scowcroft, both key NSC figures.

In the midst of the energy discussions at the White House in which Helms and Jim were involved, Ehrlichman suddenly told Helms his successor would be sworn in the following morning. On the way back to the agency, Helms was fuming and said, "That son of a bitch could have told me earlier. It's typical of him." A short time later, the president met with Helms and told him he would regard him the first among equals among ambassadors involved in the Middle East and asked Helms to prepare an overall view of the problems of the time. Jim actually prepared this paper for Helms, one of his last assignments for Dick before he moved on to Iran.

The White House job initially was one of briefing new appointees on the Middle East and energy. Jim briefed cabinet appointees such the new Treasury Secretary George Shultz, Bill Simon, Ken Van Damm, and numerous others. In between, Jim worked on drafts of an energy policy and stayed in touch with Senator Jackson. During this period, Jim traveled to the Middle East repeatedly and once visited Helms in Teheran and as a guest of the NIOC visited all its oil facilities including Kharg Island, the big producing field, and the enormous refinery at Khorrarmshar. He also met with the shah of Iran on that trip. The shah told Jim pointedly to get his Saudi friends in line, that the Oil Minister Zaki Yamani was giving him trouble. That was a tall order; it is difficult to get someone like Zaki Yamani "in line."

Jim continued to juggle these three jobs for the rest of 1973 and on into 1974 with Watergate becoming a more menacing factor. Then one day he went to the White House and found that Ehrlichman was gone. The whole White House staff had fallen apart under the pressures of Watergate. Henry Kissinger resigned as NSC secretary and became secretary of state. No one cared about energy any longer; it was strictly internal politics.

By that time, twenty-six years had passed since Jim had left the US Army and moved to the CIA. By his own doing, he had somewhat isolated himself in his project dealing with energy and other basic resources and was in fact spending more and more time outside the agency than in. He took a look at the project and decided it was time to pass it on either to sink or swim on its own merits. His relations with the current director, William Colby, were just so-so, and he found that he was enjoying life more on the outside than on the inside. So he retired in June 1974.

Twenty-three years later, Jim was one of fifty former officers to receive the CIA Trailblazer Award at the fiftieth anniversary on September 18, 1997. His citation read:

> Mr. Critchfield established complex and sensitive relations with counterparts in the West German intelligence services when that country emerged from the status of an occupied nation to become a sovereign power. He possessed a deep knowledge of central European matters including an encyclopedic knowledge of the German military and its intelligence personalities. Critchfield later concentrated with great distinction on Middle East issues, particularly petroleum matters and the management of clandestine operations in the region.

Critchfield receives Trailblazer Award

But he did not immediately leave government service. He continued to serve as an unpaid adviser to the chief of naval operations and would serve on its executive panel for many years. He also accepted a position as an energy adviser to Secretary Kissinger and established an office adjacent to the assistant secretary of economic affairs, Tom Enders, and continued contacts with key personalities in the oil world and the Middle East.

After awhile, he became bored with writing position papers for State and began considering setting up his own business. Then along came Nicholas Boryatinski, president of a California engineering firm based in Pasadena known as Tetra Tech Inc. And, as Bogey said to the police inspector at the end of the movie *Casablanca*, "Louis, I think this is the beginning of a beautiful friendship." Jim and Nick formed a friendship that resulted in sending his life off in yet another interesting direction.

FAMILY UPDATE

But the story is getting ahead of the family story. Bannockburn, as mentioned earlier, had become a victim of urban sprawl. Jim held on to it as long as he could, but the inevitable day came when he had to let it go. It was sold in 1973. Along with the breakup of Bannockburn came the breakup of Louise and Jim's marriage. Louise and Tom moved to McLean; Betsy and Jim moved to a small house on a friend's farm near Leesburg. Jim also rented a furnished place in Georgetown and commuted back and forth from Leesburg. In 1974, Jim and Louise were divorced.

No one wishes to highlight stressful times, particularly the author, so suffice it to say that life went on, as it inevitably does, and the era of Bannockburn would forever after become part of the memory book of life, with different meanings no doubt to all who inhabited it.

Both Ann and Jim Jr. by that time had long since flown the nest. Ann and husband Dan had recently returned from a tour of duty in Greece and settled in old Clifton with Danny, Lisa, and baby Vicki. Jim Jr. was divorced from his young wife, Priscilla (Patsy), and son Jimmy III was being raised by Patsy in southern California. Jim Jr. married Gail, a New Englander whom he had met while both were teaching school. Jim and Gail were in Chicago, where Jim was attending the School of Chiropractic Medicine.

A NEW DIRECTION: THE
TETRATECH EXPERIENCE

I guess one could say that Nicholas Boryatinski was heaven-sent. But he actually came from Russia. He was a Russian of the old aristocratic school, whose genealogy traced to Czar Nicholas, and who after the Russian Revolution was, with his two sisters, spirited out of Russia by a clever aunt who lived in London and had the proper connections to get them safely away from the Communists. Nicholas was studying physics and engineering at the University of Moscow. At the age of eighteen he entered the University of California at Berkeley; he spoke no English. Fortunately, working in the field of mathematics and science, he was able to demonstrate his brilliance sufficiently to keep his professors interested. He quickly, of course, learned English. He graduated, entered the workforce, and did very well in the field of aviation engineering.

Eventually, he pursued a long-held dream of forming his own company, and Tetra Tech was formed in 1966 by five engineers of varying backgrounds—one Chinese, two French, one Anglo-Saxon, and himself. The company engaged in water engineering, oil engineering, ports and harbors, and extremely innovative underwater research and development. Tetra Tech developed one of the first underwater remote-control cameras to be used at extreme depths for detecting faults in undersea pipelines. The company had a Rosslyn office, which dealt principally with the US Navy on a variety of classified projects around the world. Jim met Nicholas through Donald Jameson, a CIA expert on Soviet espionage cases for many years. Jamie, an Annapolis graduate who had to abandon his navy career early on because of polio, knew, it seems, every important Russian émigré in the United States. He was particularly fond of Nicholas and thought that with their joint interests in energy and the navy, Nicholas and Jim would hit it off. Well, they did, and Nick soon offered Jim a desk in his Tetra Tech office in Rosslyn to pursue his interest in energy research. Before long, Jim and Nick worked out an arrangement whereby Jim would organize Tetra Tech International Inc. (TtI) to pursue business in the Middle East. He also made Jim a vice president of Tetra Tech Inc. with the option to purchase company stock. This was what we mean by heaven-sent, because now Jim had a base on which to build a future. He didn't have any money, mind you, but he had the base.

It was around this time that Jim started asking me out for dinners. I had recently broken a long-term relationship and was unencumbered. I knew, of course, that Jim was fascinating, having worked for him for six years. On

December 4, 1975, Jim and I were married at the home of my brother and sister-in-law, Bruce and Margie Matthews, with a small group of the closest friends and family in attendance. Everyone there seemed happy, particularly my mother, who always fretted about my not settling down. She needed to fret no longer. I loved Jim. Everyone did.

THE OMAN EXPERIENCE

Shortly after Tetra Tech International Inc. was formed, Jim flew to London and Oman, first to meet with close advisers to Sultan Qaboos and then to meet with the sultan himself. There is no denying that he had known many of these people throughout his years as chief of NE Division and the subsequent energy project of which he was head. It mattered little to them that Jim had left the CIA behind. They liked what they saw in Tetra Tech and had a rather amazing attachment to Jim. For some of these people, he was a father figure. One of his closest Saudi friends, a man of considerable wealth and prestige, continued to call him "Sir" even though they were on an equal footing business wise.

The Oman story would one day be published as a book.[4] To this end, Jim had saved all the key files from Tetra Tech International, much to Lois's chagrin. But there was definitely plenty of material for a fascinating story, and little did I know at the time that I would end up authoring the book. It is too long a story to tell here. It spans almost fifteen years from beginning to end. But I will tell a bit of it.

The first major contract TtI obtained involved becoming the advisory group to the Sultanate of Oman on the development of Oman's energy resources. TtI employees sat on the Oman side of the negotiating table in dealing with British Shell Oil Company, which was producing Oman's oil at that time. The first permanent employee of TtI was Ken Bodine. Ken and Pat had worked in Libya and Kuwait previously. Ken was both a lawyer and an oil geologist. Ken's office was in the Ministry of Petroleum. Both Ken and Pat were perfect fits socially. They got to know everyone and were the host and hostess with the mostest in Oman, just as the Lucids were in Bavaria. They went to Oman for a tour and stayed for ten years.

Most people felt that way about Oman. It was such a congenial country that no one wanted to leave it. The second couple to arrive in Oman was Nga and Kirk Agon. Their job was to set up a TtI office in Muscat that would oversee the care and feeding of the myriad of engineers that would be traveling in and out of and/or living in Oman. Nga and Kirk were casualties of Vietnam, Nga, a native, and Kirk, in business there, were among the many that left during the final American withdrawal. They also became popular figures in Oman; they stayed eight years.

Business expanded quickly. Soon, there were four TtI teams working on projects in Oman. There was the oil and gas project; a water resources project; a regional development project, which dealt with land use and infrastructure building; and the Musandam Peninsula project. The Musandam Peninsula sat on the strategic Hormuz Strait, the entryway to the Persian Gulf, through which much of the world's oil flowed. Up until TtI got involved, about the only structure at Musandam was a military outpost guarding a two-thousand-foot dirt runway. Feudal tribes who seemed to be always feuding inhabited it. TtI moved in to develop the area, and soon a new town was built and a civilian government was put in place. Even the tribesmen were happy. They were prospering, and once and for all, they did not have to migrate each season in search of water. TtI engineers and administrators lived on the spot while the town was being laid out and built. Some were American, some were British, and most were adventurous.

THE BEACH HOUSE

Life was not all work. In fact, "life was a beach." Borrowing money and throwing caution to the winds, Jim and I built a wonderful beach house on the Outer Banks in Southern Shores in 1979. In those days, it was the trend to rent your home during the summer months, making the project self-sustaining. And that is what happened for five years. After that, with more dollars in the bank, we took the house off the market, and it became and still is a gathering place for family and friends. Easter, Memorial Day, Fourth of July, and Labor Day are particularly popular.

But from the beginning, Thanksgiving became the tradition. And for our good friends Rose and John Bannigan, it became so for them as well. They built a second home in Southern Shores in 1980. Even John's daughter and family come from California to celebrate Thanksgiving. It started when the Websters came down for Thanksgiving in 1979, and Lisa declared with some firmness that this would now be a family tradition. Everyone loved the beach, the dunes, the sound, but Lisa seemed to have an extra special feeling for the place that never waned. Except when she was in Germany, she never missed a Thanksgiving, even one year coming all the way from college in Arkansas, suffering through the hurly burly of crowded airports to get there. It is our greatest tragedy that she lost her life there during a family gathering in June of 1992. She died from a drowning accident in the Currituck Sound.

Typical Thanksgiving

The place was special also for Bill Critchfield. Up until his death, he visited at least once a year. He walked the beach for miles, stopped along the way to read and dream, lunched in Duck, and treated everyone to dinner at the Sanderling Inn. Pat practiced his first long speech with Ann coaching him as they walked miles down the beach. Danny evolved into our erstwhile tree keeper. When we built our house, it was on sand only. Not one plant and not one tree. After a few years, while Danny was growing up, it became a forest of live oak and bayberry intertwined with grape and brambles. By that time, Danny, with a good set of muscles and unsuspecting friends invited down for weekends, turned our overgrown forest into a beautiful park, clearing out all the underbrush and making it truly a beautiful place. Vicki grew from a little girl who loved the waves to a beautiful girl with lofty ideals and a good heart. Vicki will always remember that the beach was where she had her first full-time job at age fifteen at the ice cream parlor in Duck.

The beach has also been important in later years for Jim, the writer. Much of the best work he did on his German book was done there. The Duck room became his writing hideaway. And while he was working in the Duck Room, I started this story on my computer sitting at the kitchen counter. He finished his. I continued to work on mine.

BACK TO BUSINESS IN OMAN

Jim never lived in Oman. He ran the business out of Rosslyn and traveled to Oman about every two months. He would stay there two to three weeks and, while there, traveled to all the remote areas where TtI was working. At the peak of its business, the company had about two hundred employees in Oman, and its annual revenues totaled $10 million. Employees were mainly Americans and British, but a large number of Indians were holding down administrative positions.

Inevitably, there were news reports that the CIA backed this major development activity in Oman, because of Oman's strategic position. How far from the truth this was. After he left the CIA, not one CIA official ever contacted him about TtI's activities in Oman. In fact, many years later when Jim met Bill Casey at a social function, Casey remarked to him, "Oh, yes, Jim Critchfield. You are the man who proved there was a life after CIA." But the press had a hard time letting go of this myth. Even the *Washington Post*'s ombudsman on April 1, 1986 took to task a *Post* correspondent who had written an article insinuating that Jim and TtI were part of the CIA in Oman. He said that he had not seen a person indicted by the use of language this way in some time. After that, the articles stopped. Kirk Agon had his share of indictments too. Perhaps because he looked so much like

Robert Redford, people in Oman were also saying that the true CIA chief of station in Oman was Kirk. The real chief, who was ensconced quietly in the American Embassy, was no doubt chagrined at this. I used to tease Kirk that when he was in Washington, he should go to the CIA and demand his "retirement pay," since everyone seemed to think he was on the CIA roster.

Back in California, Nicholas was doing some fast footwork that resulted in the sale of Tetra Tech Inc. to Honeywell Inc. of Minneapolis. This too was heaven-sent, because a share of Tetra Tech stock was expected to fall to about $5 a share from its high of around $30. When the buyout took place and Tetra Tech stock was exchanged for Honeywell stock, it was suddenly worth $58 a share. That was the good news. The bad news was that Honeywell never really could find a place for all the component parts of Tetra Tech Inc., including TtI. Jim had excellent relations with Honeywell management, but the company was in the business of selling defense weapons and control systems, not oil and water engineering projects. Back and forth and back and forth went TtI and Honeywell, until finally a very amicable settlement was made wherein Jim bought out TtI from Honeywell, paying for it on the installment plan, so to speak. In 1985, he became sole owner of TtI.

By 1988, the sultan was dedicated to a program of "Omanization." His aggressive education of young Omanis since 1970 was beginning to produce enough talent so that Oman did not have to rely on expatriates to run the country, which was how business got done up until then. More and more, the sultan indicated he wanted to turn some of TtI's projects over to Omani control, and in fact many of them were transferred to Omani ministries, although many had also been completed. In addition to this rather lofty Omani policy, on the oil scene there were other groups that were slowly making inroads into TtI's territory. A well-known Dutch oil trader, John Deuss, flew into Oman offering his style of aggressive advice and claiming he could make more money for Oman than TtI could. There were many other factors at play here too numerous to fit into this equation, but suffice it say that after a very successful decade and a half, TtI's activities in Oman were phased out. In 1988, in recognition of his years of service to Oman, the sultan presented Jim with its highest civilian medal, the Order of the Star of Oman. Jim was seventy-one years of age. John Sasser, who had been running the Oman projects for TtI for some five years, received a medal at the same time.

HM Sultan Qaboos giving Jim award

GULF FUTURES INC.

Before the TtI presence in Oman was phased out, Jim decided to move the office from Rosslyn to McLean, into smaller quarters. He purchased the third floor of an office condominium on Whittier Avenue. This was in 1987. There was a small staff: Ralph Redford, Lee Miller, Bill Creighton, Arthur Rypinski, John Bannigan, and Lois, who joined the staff as a researcher for a pittance pay. After her retirement from the agency in 1982, she had set up a home office doing the odd research job for some clients but making little at it. So joining Jim's group was no economic sacrifice. While TtI was still operating, Jim in 1985 formed another company, called Gulf Futures Inc. In his words, it was a mechanism to study and analyze the era of oil, and it was for Gulf Futures Inc. that the McLean staff worked, publishing a monthly newsletter for a small group of clients who were willing to pay enough annually to keep the newsletter in the black.

Gulf Futures Inc. also became involved in a horse racing operation centered around horse trainer Betsy, and despite the hard work involved and infusion of considerable of the company's capital, the business failed and was shut down.

It was at about this time that Jim decided put the McLean office on the market. It became clear that even that small office was not needed to produce the monthly newsletter. And we had taken a big step by deciding to move to the country. After we were married in 1975, we lived in a two-bedroom apartment at the Foxhall on Massachusetts Avenue near American University. In 1980 we sold that apartment, when real estate was inflated, and took that money and purchased a townhouse in Madison of McLean, only one mile from my office. Then in 1986, we bought fourteen acres at the foothills of the Blue Ridge in Delaplane, Virginia, near Scuffleburg and after dillying around for a year decided to build onto the small house that was on this property. A beautiful home— a sort of English country home—was built that was designed mainly by Jim. We moved there in September 1988. We sold the McLean home just before the real estate market collapsed and realized a 100 percent profit on it. Talk about Lady Luck!

After moving to Delaplane, the commute to and from McLean became more and more of a nuisance. Also, we realized that we could probably reduce the Gulf Futures activity to a mom-and-pop operation run with computers, a fax, and a Xerox machine and printer out of a home office in Scuffleburg. And that is what happened. The McLean office was sold; the employees, who have all remained friends, retired, and another era came to a close. We continued writing the newsletter for two more years and then phased it out.

LIFE IN SCUFFLEBURG

Jim threw himself into the beautification of Scuffleburg Junction—our nickname for the property. The area was called Scuffleburg back in the 1800s. White fences appeared; trees, bushes, and flowers were planted; the fields were cut; the fallen-down stone wall along the front of the road was rebuilt, stone by stone; and the pond was rehabilitated by the rebuilding of the dam, a project engineered and built solely by Jim. All of a sudden, we noticed, the neighbors began sprucing up their properties.

Across from the house is a Civil War era Baptist church, built in 1845. This charming brick structure is framed in our living room windows by design. It gives one a great sense of peace to look out on it. It sits in an oak grove of trees that date back to George Washington. In fact, he could have surveyed this land, for all we know. The road in front of our house leads to the village of Scuffleburg. When we moved there its population was four. Its population increased to five with the birth of Dean Janka. By 1995, the population of Scuffleburg numbered seven. Scuffleburg was one of the locations where John Mosby and his famous raiders hid out between skirmishes with the Yankees. The history of the name Scuffleburg is not known, but most say it got its name because one had to scuffle in and scuffle out of it. Of the three houses there, one was owned by a man named Martin, who was the last member of the jury to vote for the execution of John Brown in Harpers Ferry. The Martin house dates back to the late 1700s. When we moved there it was the weekend retreat of the Janka family, with whom we became good friends.

Directly across from the front entrance of our old house is the Ashby farm. The Ashby family distinguished itself in several military campaigns dating back to the Revolutionary War, the War of 1812, and the Civil War. Beside the house is a stone structure that was the slave quarters during Civil War times and before. Next to the road is the Ashby cemetery, which has been restored. In it many of the Ashby officers are buried. Only General Turner Ashby is missing. His remains are buried in the cemetery in Winchester. Turner Ashby lost his life in battle the day after he was promoted from colonel to general. There is a story that before he left for war, he buried much of the family silver near the homestead, and no one knew where it was. It remains buried, perhaps, who knows, on our property. Our piece of land was formerly part of the Ashby land.

FAMILY UPDATE II

Jim took pride in the fact that when asked about his children, he could tell friends that all four lived within one hour of him. That was in the early 1990s.

Ann and Dan were in Clifton, less than an hour east of Scuffleburg. Ann distinguished herself by going back to the university and getting a degree in accounting followed by passing the CPA exam on the first sitting; those in the field know this is no small feat. They had a tour of duty in Frankfurt, where Ann worked at Chemical Bank. Dan had a tour in New Delhi as chief; Ann kept the home open and pursued a challenging job at the software company Legent.

Jim Jr. and wife Lisa had a chiropractic practice in Culpeper, less than an hour in the opposite direction. In between producing three children—Travis, Connie, and Brittany—and being a father as well to Lisa's son, Adam, Jim continued to build airplanes and pursue interests in deep-sea treasure hunting. Lisa, an accomplished sportswoman, made sure that the children learned sports at the earliest possible age. They all became accomplished skiers and swimmers. And Jim III, from California, who visited during the summer of 1994 prior to going to Bolivia for two years with the Peace Corps, extended the hand of friendship to his stepsiblings. It was the first time he had met his father, who had left Pat and him at birth. It was a poignant and perhaps difficult moment. Jim III graduated from UC Berkeley and did a stint with the Forestry Service in California, Oregon, and Washington before signing on with the Peace Corps. While in Bolivia he helped the local area with reforestation and teaching an environmental education course in Spanish at the local schools. While in the Peace Corps, he met and later married Suzanne Takeuchi, also from California. Both were studying at the University of Arizona, and Jim and Lois attended their graduation.

Betsy and her mother lived less than an hour north of Scuffleburg, where Betsy pursued horse training and trading. No matter where she lived, she surrounded herself with a menagerie of horses, dogs, cats, pheasants, goats, chickens, and I don't know what else. She was totally dedicated to the business of the horse.

Tom, a city dweller first in Falls Church and currently in Reston, was another hour farther east toward Washington. An engineer now retired from the Department of the Army, he pursued a myriad of sports, including skiing. He and Jim spent a week in Aspen during the winter of 1993. He maintains his interest in music and is the family pianist.

Another tradition of those days was that all of the above would gather at the Scuffleburg homestead around Christmas every year for the buckwheat pancake breakfast. No one made buckwheats like Jim did. He learned it from his mother. They are great. I would add a few side dishes and mimosas, and it became a nice event. Sometimes, this was the only occasion when all the siblings were together at the same time during the year.

Tom, Betsy, Jim, Ann and Jim Jr.

GERMANY: FROM ENEMY TO ALLY

Until one gets into book writing, you don't realize how all-consuming it can be. Jim worked on his story off and on for years, but in 1993 it began in earnest. He would write and rewrite several hours a day. Research and eyewitness accounts from former colleagues were ongoing. There were three trips to Germany, one to Canada, and many trips back and forth to the Outer Banks, carrying computers and equipment with us, to write, write, write. The book begins when the war in Europe ended and traces the movement of the enemy Germany to the time when it was accepted into the NATO alliance.

There were some unwelcome interruptions in this work. First, after cataract surgery in 1991, Jim was diagnosed with macular degeneration in both eyes. That is a condition of the retina whereby the frontal vision is affected. When reading a page from a book, for example, one sees a blank circle in the middle, instead of print. At its worst stage, reading and driving a car is impossible, but one's peripheral vision remains intact. A laser operation on one eye stopped the spread of the condition, but sadly, there was and still is no cure for it. As a result of this, Jim was forced to change his method of book research. A number of friends began reading research material onto tapes; others did German translations of important material, and Library of Congress books on tape took the place of the books themselves. Working on the computer, for some reason, was still possible with some adjustments to the computer monitor. And finally, in 1995 we were made aware of an electronic reader that, like a computer, put the image of the printed page on a computer-type screen, and, once again, Jim was able to read. Therefore, a combination of all these aides kept the book moving forward toward completion.

In the late summer of 1992, after our trip to England, Wales, and Germany, during a routine check with the ophthalmologist, Jim told him of a blackout incident that had occurred during the night before. Dr. Arnold Oshinsky got a strange look, questioned Jim further and then sent him immediately to a vascular surgeon for a Doppler exam. When we got home that night, the surgeon, Dr. Stanley Crossland, phoned with the bad news of carotid artery blockage, 95–99 percent. We returned the next day to Northern Virginia Doctors Hospital for an MRI, and the next day, Jim was scheduled for surgery. None of us had time to think, which was just as well, but by 1:00 a.m. the doctor had successfully performed surgery on the most severely blocked artery. Three months later, he operated on the other side. We owe Dr. Oshinsky, in particular, much credit for recognizing this dangerous condition. And Dr. Crossland, in our minds, is a saint in surgeon's clothes. They both were truly lifesavers.

We learned so much from this experience. For one thing, we now know that this condition is hereditary. My research on the Critchfield family has revealed beyond the question of a doubt that the death of Grandfather Henry Hardesty Critchfield, at age forty-three, was from a brain hemorrhage, no doubt brought on by a stroke. The cause of death of Jim's father at age forty-eight was pneumonia and "labor." This could have stroke implications. And Jim's great-grandfather on his mother's side died from "paralysis"—read *stroke*. An autopsy conducted on Pat revealed carotid artery blockage. Pat was sixty-three when he died from a stroke. Dr. Crossland strongly recommended that all family members over the age of fifty have routine Doppler examinations of the carotid arteries annually. Are you listening?

MOVE TO THE JAMES RIVER

It happened almost overnight. One weekend in the fall of 1995, when we were driving to the beach house, I suggested a detour in Williamsburg. This was not a totally innocent act. I had seen an ad in a Virginia magazine for a new community being built on the James River near Williamsburg. We drove in and were greeted by a Governor's Land salesman, who it turns out was a CIA brat, Jim Parker, whose father had been a senior administrative official during our time. Jim Parker showed us around Governor's Land, spending most of his time talking about his father, but after several hours we landed up on a piece of property right on the James River. We had to get there by four-wheel-drive because it had not yet been developed. The view was spectacular. So to make a long story short, we put $10,000 down on it with a promise to buy and headed out to the Outer Banks. Driving through Williamsburg on our way out, we spotted our granddaughter Vicki preparing for a run down Duke of Gloucester Street. Needless to say, she was astonished to hear that we had been property shopping. But a year later, she claimed a bedroom at 1552 Harbor Road for her last semester at the College of William and Mary. Construction on the house was completed in August 1996, and we settled in. We sold the farm at Scuffleburg to our friends and local residents Harry and Susan Huberth. Harry and Jim served together during WW II and had become reacquainted the year before.

LIVING ON THE JAMES
RIVER: 1996–2003

Governors Land turned out to be a most welcoming neighborhood. Many couples were coming from the surrounding areas near Washington, DC, and New York City, had recently retired, and were relocating to Williamsburg for many of the same reasons we did. We soon realized that something was missing in our lifestyle. Yes, of course—a boat! Jim had always loved boats going back to the days in Germany when he taught Ann and Jim Jr. to sail on Lake Starnberg. One fine day, a Virginia Beach boat show came to the Marina, and there it was, a brand new twenty-two-foot powerboat ready to go. All it needed was a name. Lois had a brainstorm, and *Tinker Tailor* was christened shortly after our check cleared the seller. Why *Tinker Tailor*? Do you recall John Le Carre's spy thriller *Tinker Tailor Soldier Spy*? What better captain of *Tinker Tailor* than soldier and spy Jim Critchfield! Get it?

Tinker Tailor with its Captain

Friday Night Party

So in addition to our wonderful new neighbors and our Friday night cocktail parties, we spent many hours with our boating friends exploring the James River. Many, of course, were neighbors, because most Harbor Road homes were on the Marina. But we soon met other boaters, and our social circle greatly expanded. We were happy with the decision to move to Governor's Land. And right outside our community was an added attraction—the College of William and Mary. It was a tremendous resource, because all of its lectures were open to the public, and it became nationally known for its outstanding lifelong learning group called the Christopher Wren Association. It was like going back to college again but without the exams. And I haven't even mentioned Jamestown, Yorktown, and Williamsburg, the birthplaces of our nation.

We continued the Thanksgiving tradition at the beach. Lois researched where to buy the largest fresh turkey available; Ann arose very early to prepare the turkey for the oven, always grumbling that it was too big or the oven was too small, and then, after several hours, Jim put on the chef's hat and began the carving ritual. We enjoyed arguing over when dinner would be served. Ann said 4:00 p.m., and Lois said 6:00 p.m. The Bannigans usually arrived around 3:30 p.m. with the potatoes ready to cook and Rose's famous pumpkin and pecan pies and her equally famous cranberry sauce and made-from-scratch applesauce. There was also the traditional photo shoot either on the deck or in front of the fireplace. These group photos, starting from the first Thanksgiving in 1979, are displayed on the downstairs wall of the beach house. The bar opened at some point; everyone was busy doing their assigned thing, and momentum picked up when Jim donned his chef's hat and John began his dramatic rendition of mashing the potatoes with a fork. Ann and Vicki were making the gravy, and Lois was completing the various vegetable dishes. Most popular were her creamed onions. Not at all popular were her Brussels sprouts, but it was tradition. There were anywhere from ten to fifteen people sitting down at an elegantly set table, including the sterling silver flatware Lois would bring from home just for this occasion. Everyone transitioned to wine, and the eating orgy began. The most fun was sitting around the table together, and many hours passed before the group disbursed.

While in Williamsburg, Jim continued to follow activities in the Middle East and travel back and forth to Washington to meet friends and abroad to attend Le Cercle meetings. Le Cercle was a sort of old boys club of mainly British and American former intelligence officers and diplomats who had served in the Middle East. There were also Europeans, both West and East; one or two Moroccans; Turks; and a few members from the Arab states. Wives were also invited to these four-day meetings, and during the 1990s, we traveled to London, Munich, Istanbul, and Washington. It was like going to a reunion.

Jim also maintained his contacts with the German Embassy and with friends in Germany. He received the Order of Merit of the Federal Republic of Germany, which is the highest award given to civilians.

Award Presentation at German Embassy

Speaking at his funeral on May 23, 2003, retired BND President Dr. Hans-Georg paid tribute to Jim, calling him a courageous pioneer of trusted and deeply routed cooperation between the two countries. Jim's engagement, he said, contributed to the emergence of a democratic and reliable partner, in particular within the NATO Alliance. Jim continued to work diligently on his German book. I helped him edit it and get it in shape to show publishers. After many rejections, the Naval Institute Press showed interest, and an agreement was struck. But fate would intervene, and Jim would never see the finished copy.

FINAL DAYS

The day after Christmas of 1999, Jim went to visit daughter Betsy and his former wife, Louise. It was a post-Christmas luncheon. We had spent Christmas at the Webster household, and he wished to share time with those he had not been with on Christmas Day. Son Tom drove him to their country home, and as Jim described it to me, they had a pleasant time looking around the farm and having lunch. But something went wrong. I am not sure what happened, but there was what I would describe as a "sibling explosion." Whatever triggered it, there were verbal exchanges and tears. Jim and Tom departed.

That event profoundly affected Jim. He could not understand it, and he returned to Williamsburg with a heavy heart. It literally made him ill. In subsequent years, when he talked with physicians about his yet undiagnosed problems, he always dated the beginning of the end to that event. He was deeply troubled. It was no secret that over the years, Jim and Louise had helped Betsy get out of financial jams due to her failing horse operations. It was clear that she expected this support, and it was an ongoing source of friction among her siblings, who deeply resented this favoritism. It even prompted a heartfelt letter from Jim to all four children and Louise of his intentions to be evenhanded. He told his children in that 1998 letter, admitting he had made mistakes, that as he became older, he wanted them to know "I loved all my four children equally but found them, at different times in their lives, different from one another. You were leading different lives in different circumstances." That was his way of explaining why he dealt with each one of them separately. I will leave other private family letters for them to sort out. But after the incident in 1999, which indicated to him that his youngest daughter had not understood his declaration of equality, their relationship was never the same.

So time passed. We lived the usual life—working, writing, traveling, visiting friends and relatives, parties, entertaining, and so on. But every time Jim went to the doctor, he said, "I don't feel good."

"Oh, Jim," the doctor said, "you are just getting old. You are in better shape than most of my patients ten years younger."

"Okay, but I still don't feel good."

From 1998 to 2002, we went to a local gastroenterologist, a urologist, a cardiologist, an eye and ear specialist, and every kind of doctor you could think of. Many tests were taken. Nothing appeared. "Oh, Jim, it is just age."

Finally, in April 2002, when I picked Jim up after his latest consultation in Williamsburg about his stomach pains, he told me they said they could do nothing more. We went home, and I got on the phone to Mayo Clinic. Two weeks later, we were in the Mayo Clinic's Jacksonville campus, and a week later they told us Jim had pancreatic cancer. Our reaction was strange. We were more relieved than shocked. We finally knew what we were dealing with.

Even at that stage, Jim was still telling the doctors that this all began the day after Christmas in 1999.

Was he ready to give up? In no way. He explained to the surgeon at Mayo Clinic that he had lived a life of combat, and he was prepared to tough it out. Whatever needed to be done, he was prepared to get on with it. It never occurred to him or me that we might be going down a slippery slope toward death. We were going to get this cancer out of him and go on with our lives. The doctors were rather curious to see such a tough eighty-five-year-old, but you could also see some admiration there.

We all know what happened then. He had to have some heart work done, and that delayed the cancer surgery for more than a month. We drove back and forth to Jacksonville still hopeful and in no way depressed. It was only a mechanical thing. We would be back home in no time.

Well, of course, that did not happen. Surgery on August 1 went reasonably well, but the surgeon did have the serious message that he got 98 percent of the cancerous tumor but 2 percent was left behind. Still we did not understand. What is 2 percent? We can overcome that. But what hit us during recovery was far worse than that. A rupture, an infection, pneumonia, heart fibrillation—a nightmare in intensive care. Result: Jim lived but had to be fed intravenously and developed hospitalitis (my term), which meant that he had infections one after the other. We despaired; we thought we would never get out of there. Jim looked upon it as a prison run by Saddam Hussein's henchmen.

But we escaped five weeks later and came home in a twin engine Cessna with two medics on board. We landed at Williamsburg airport, and life all of a sudden became whole again. Well, almost whole. Our wonderful friends settled us back into our home, but still Jim, damaged from the experience, was receiving sustenance via a feeding tube in the stomach and antibiotics still fighting the infections. We had twenty-four-hour nursing care and a lot of anguish. But Jim never complained—well, almost never complained. He was the most forgiving patient I have ever known. He was so happy to be home.

As time passed, Jim improved, and we thought we were really on the road to recovery. We got the book manuscript to the publishers, visited with friends, and worked on walking and getting out of doors. By December, things were so good that we attended two meetings in Washington and Christmas with children, and in January Jim even did an interview with BBC in Washington and had an article published in the *Wall Street Journal* on his favorite subject, Iraq and the occupation. We were on easy street.

We had returned to Mayo Clinic in December for another CT scan. That was an important event. Jim was so determined to show the doctors that the man who left on a stretcher was back with only a cane for support.

But the films did not lie. There again it showed another small growth. We thought, oh, that is not bad. But I will never forget when we left the consultation room, the surgeon and his team turned and went down the hall in one direction, and we went in the opposite direction. I looked over my shoulder and saw our surgeon's shoulders somewhat slumped down. I could only read into that his disappointment. He knew. We still didn't.

From September to April, we were in the hands of such wonderful friends. Dr. Jerry Broock came almost every evening to sit with Jim and discuss world events. Fern Broock was ultrasupportive. Louisa Ford would stop in and offer her positive and cheerful thoughts. Sean Fitzpatrick read poetry. Bill Spaller dropped in with questions on the Middle East. Also there were Elaine Spaller, Sue Ellen Fitzpatrick, Ross Ford, Lee and Ned Thoet, Joni and Sandy Whitwell, Ed Roesch and Fay Shealy, Betsy and Boyd McKelvain, Bettie and Wayne Wright, Louise and Gerry Smith, and Lee and Paula Hougen. The list goes on. His doctors suggested we do chemotherapy, but we would wait for three months to get another reading. Neither Jim nor I really wanted him to do chemo. It was not considered a cure but a palliative treatment. Something told us he had been through enough. But still we were not talking about dying. That was not in the cards for us. Jim still had too much to do.

We had many visits. James Critchfield Jr. and James Critchfield III. They came separately. This father and son had not bonded. Tom came for his traditional Super Bowl evening; they bonded. Ann continued her trek that began in Jacksonville and went on to the end. Betsy was in tears, knowing that death was inevitable but not wanting to face it. It was a busy time between January and April.

I am the first to tell you that I did not wish to face it. We had so many episodes that should have told us what was coming. But interestingly, even Dr. Connell, who became our good friend making house calls and having coffee and conversation with Jim, kept trying to find solutions that would prolong Jim's life. We wanted to keep this man alive!

After Jim III left to return to California, we began to have problems. Jim had dizzy spells and had to sit for a time before rising to walk. (Did he need to see an ear specialist—perhaps he had an inner ear problem?). Some days he felt grumpy and depressed. (Louisa found a company that produces light boxes for those who are sunshine deprived during long winters. Maybe we should try that; maybe we could all try it.) On walks, he tired before being able to make it back home. (He needs to eat more to gain strength). He fell while taking a shower. (Did he slip on the floor?) I can't tell you how we rationalized every incident. We never considered that it was the cancer that was attacking his system. Never. Nor did he. When we had to call for help, the medics said they thought Jim needed to be checked out in the hospital. He said: "No, this will pass." But it did not pass.

On March 31, we checked into the emergency room at Williamsburg Community Hospital. A few days there and he stabilized, so we went home. In mid-April, we went back, and Jim told neighbor Elaine, who was visiting, "I am never going to get out of here." Despite our protestations, he was correct. Those were amazing days. Day by day, we held hands and went through interminable procedures to prolong life. Sean, Sue Ellen, Louisa, Ross, Bill, Elaine, Jerry, and Fern in and out, in and out. We still could not face death. Pneumonia set in. Children came. Friends were there every day. CIA colleague and my former boss Dick Stolz came and read from Richard Helms's biography quoting Jim. Jim heard that. Jerry would come and put his hands on Jim's shoulders and shake him gently, saying, "We love you, Jim." He heard it all, and he was wonderful in his responses. He thanked every nurse, every aide, and every person who came to help. He was the most gentle man I have every observed. Even approaching death, he made friends out of strangers.

Finally, Dr. Mark Ellis, the oncologist, shocked me into reality. He said: it is over. It is only a matter of days. In come the angels from Hospice House. On April 22, the decision was made to move Jim there. Ann was with me, and I said to her, "I couldn't stand to see your father jostled one more time from one stretcher to another. Let them do it, and we will meet them at the Hospice House." Ann and I then went, of all places, to the Cities Grille for lunch and actually had a nice lunch with a glass of wine. If Jim had died while I was drinking wine, I never would have forgiven myself. I phoned whomever I could reach, and at 2:00 p.m. we arrived at the Hospice House just as the ambulance was bringing Jim to the door. I could not bring myself to look—too many ambulance trips and too many transfers. Then we entered this beautiful place—a piece of heaven. I had never seen anything like it before. While I signed the innumerable papers for admission, they settled Jim into his room. It was like a stepping-stone to heaven. To this day, I can't believe it. The room looked out onto a patio with gardens and trees in the distance. So peaceful. Before I knew it, Louisa had arrived and then Bill and Elaine. We all stayed with him and talked to him about who was there and how much we loved him. We said a prayer, and then he just sighed and quit breathing, holding my hand. It was so quiet and so sudden. I had no time to even say, "Come back; come back." There would be no coming back. We had only been there two hours.

Arlington Cemetery

Jim was laid to rest in beautiful Arlington Cemetery on May 23. Everyone then resumed their normal lives, each grieving in his own way. Lois, very much alone and with time to spare, sat down at the computer one day and wrote this imaginary letter from Jim to her. It made her feel better.

Letter from a soul mate written circa August 2003

Dear Lois,

I am truly sorry I had to leave you. The body just gave out. It broke down and was beyond repair, as you well know. My departure was not so bad, was it? At least we were holding hands. But I want you to know, Lois, that although my body quit, my spirit and soul did not. Like it or not, I am still around. I think you know that. When you awake in the morning, I am there to comfort you. I hope you can feel my warmth around your shoulders. And when you seem particularly lazy, I give you a little push to get up and get going. Yes, that is I. There is so much to do, and you do it so well. You just need a little push from me to get going. That is no sin. Some people are just night owls, and I know you are one of those.

As usual, you have too many balls in the air, but I know nothing will slow you down until you have completed your work. You have carried a large burden this past year. I kept telling you that, but you would just smile and say you couldn't imagine doing it any other way. I am sorry I was not as appreciative of your efforts in preparing all those elegant dinners for me. I surprised myself by liking peanut butter and ice cream cups more than your wonderful cooking. When the body gives up, it clearly does so by retrograding to the point of wanting nothing at all. I remember your sigh of resignation when you returned my hospital trays of untouched foods. Those trays were not important; your presence was.

I am writing this to you because I am not able to be with you all the time. In the beginning there is much to do, much ground (perhaps space is a better word) to cover. But I want you to know that you are the most important mortal around. I always thought you were. I have been watching, and I certainly am proud of how you are handling my affairs. You really don't have to make an icon out of me! I never was one in life, but I have to admit I rather enjoy some of the tributes paid to me. I had such a wonderfully active life, and it is good to know that I may have contributed at least something to a better world. Although the world I left was pretty chaotic, there is hope it will settle down, and perhaps some of my thoughts will rise to the surface and form a base.

As for my children, I have to say that there are no surprises there. They are all performing as I would have expected. Ann stands by your side providing all the support you need but stands back when you need space. Her loyalty to you is without question. Tom surfaces every so often to check in. I wish he would find a soul mate. I used to tell him how much he was missing by not experiencing the wonders of marriage. Jim, my most self-centered son, needs to rise above himself. Tell him things are not that intense out here. And also tell him he does not have all the answers. Betsy could also use that advice. She simply wore me out. Somewhere in my computer there are dozens of letters I sent to her about life's responsibilities, but she ignored them. I know she is grieving. All I wanted was peace and quiet; I finally got it. Now they have to get on with their lives. I have no more to say on that score.

A few words about grandchildren. I was thrilled with the arrival of James Traylor Lyon and await news of the new Webster in the coming months. These children are blessed with loving parents and will have many adventures in life. I think in your many photo albums there are some great pictures of me with Vicki and Bobbie indicating how I felt about them. I loved them both. Vicki's time with us during her last year of college was special, wasn't it? Do you think she gives me just a little bit of credit for her excellent speech-making? And as for that, is there a grandfather in the world more proud than I of the eulogy Dan gave? All their visits during the tough times gave me happiness. James III saw me at my best. We had some quality time together, and I know life will treat him well, as he so richly deserves.

I want to add a few remarks here. When we arrived home from Mayo Clinic, I on a stretcher and you by my side, I was astonished to find our friends at planeside and at home getting me settled in. Let's see. Sean and Jerry at the airport; Louisa, Ross, Bill, Elaine, Fern, Sue Ellen (who have I left out?) at home. And all the neighbors waving as we drove in. What did I do to deserve that? Then as the weeks and months went on, they were there, day after day. I am so devoted to Louisa with her upbeat personality coming to hold my hand and Jerry always with encouraging support. Every day Jerry was there to talk with me and keep me thinking. It was like having a whole new set of children. I loved them. Later, when we went through yet another hospital ordeal, all those friends were there to the end. I still don't think I deserved their devotion, but I reveled in it.

Before I get on to more serious subjects, there are a few matters I need to take up with you. I know you and Marcia cleaned out the garage at the beach house recently. That was very brave of you. You probably should have saved some of those cans of nails, nuts, and bolts. I bet you will be going down to Ace Hardware soon to buy replacements when all you would have had to do is look in one of those rusty cans. But I was proud of you that before you threw away all those keys, you found the one to Ann's little red case. That little red case was Ann's pride and joy when we boarded the Holland American line in 1948 to go live in Germany. The case is long gone, but she will love the key. You can throw away the key to Weedie's blue hatbox. I can't tell you where the antique "Herren Komode" is, but aren't the four keys for it works of art? And didn't I warn you not to throw away any box before looking in it? Weren't you surprised to find my World War II gun-cleaning metal box complete with implements? I carried it in my backpack from the landing in southern France in August 1944 until VE Day, May 1945. Please give it to Sean, the founder of OGG (Old Guys with Guns) with my compliments.

I know what you are thinking. Cleaning out the garage was child's play compared to what is facing you at home. One garage, two attics, two closets (you own the other four; maybe now our guests will have some place to hang their clothes!), not to speak of dresser drawers. Can't face it, can you? Well, I can't say I blame you. I have noticed, though, that you have begun to sneak some of your winter clothes into my space, just pushing my things unceremoniously aside. Well, you have some options here. You can just leave my things where they are until you join me, and then the children can do the honors. But if you do that, think of all the fun you will miss by discovering all those locked boxes (for which you have already thrown away the keys) and finding out what treasures are inside of them.

But save that for a rainy day. I want you to go out and enjoy yourself—be with our friends and relax.

Perhaps this is a good place to make a few comments about drinking. You have my permission to open the last bottle of 1971 Mouton Rothschild—the last of the case given to us as a wedding gift. But go easy on my Black Label. That was a Christmas gift from Dan last year.

As long as I am in the mode of giving orders, you have my permission to fly first class anywhere you travel. I have taken good care of my children, and I know you will take good care of our grandchildren. Just remember you are a great grandmother now, so save enough for them. And when you are sitting in first class, you may have a double martini, one for you and one for me.

But back to more serious issues. I would agree the world is in a rather chaotic state due in part to at least three totalitarian regimes (North Korea, China, and Iran) with (dare I say it?) weapons of mass destruction. These coupled with all those many nations without governments at all, namely in Africa, make for a rather sad planet. But remember how the planet looked in 1945? Remember in particular the sorry state Germany was in when the victors arrived? The year 1946 was the coldest Europe had experienced in hundreds of years; its people were barely making it on a 800 calorie diet, trains did not run, telephones did not work, and cities had been bombed into rubble. Double that with Japan after two atomic bombs, and that is chaos. Then along came the Americans, the Brits, and the Marshall Plan. Years of reconstruction, patience, and goodwill among men brought the planet back to life.

The keyword here is patience. Patience is a virtue associated with hard work, diligence, and dedication. This has nothing to do with a generation gap. Those in the field today are just as dedicated and hardworking as those of us who picked up from the ashes of WW II. They can do it; we just need to give them time and space. Why is this so difficult to understand? It is really quite simple.

Yours forever, Jim

FAMILY UPDATE III

While the foregoing was written after Jim's death and is somewhat tongue-in-cheek, it contains thoughts Jim would have written had he lived. I knew him that well. Fifteen years later, I would not change a word.

As this narrative comes to an end, I want to make this comment. I wrote this more for the great-grandchildren than for their parents, although they will benefit from learning things about their grandfather that they did not know.

For other readers who wonder whom I am talking about, these are the three wonderful grandchildren who have been so good to me. They have made my life full. They are:

Daniel Webster, son of Dan and Ann. From the early days at the beach, Dan II took the initiative to be the keeper of the trees. He is a devoted husband to wife Bobbie and great father to daughter Katie. Now fifteen, Katie has distinguished herself as a straight-A student and keen field hockey and soccer player. Bobbie's daughter Sammie also appears in family photo. She will soon graduate from the Virginia Commonwealth University in Richmond.

Vicki Lyon, daughter of Ann and Dan, a College of William and Mary graduate of whom we were very proud, and devoted wife to Eric and mother to James. James, also fifteen, is an accomplished swimmer and has just become a lifeguard. He is on the road to becoming an Eagle Scout.

James H. Critchfield III, son of Pat, and import from California along with his lovely wife, Suzanne, and the love of their lives, Olivia, who is ten years old and a talented artist.

Family photos

ONE MORE TRIBUTE

This story began with a eulogy by grandson Dan. So it is fitting to end the story with a eulogy from a friend. As noted before, Governors Land was a unique place. Friendships were as close as if everyone had lived there for many years, which was not the case. Even we residents puzzled how this was so. And those living on Harbor Road had a special bond. One day after Jim's death, these friends came to me and said they wanted to plant a tree in Jim's honor. And so they did. A bronze plaque was planted under the tree, which read: James H. Critchfield Friend, Neighbor & Patriot November 10, 2003. The tree continues to thrive today. Good friend Sean Fitzpatrick made these remarks as we gathered around the tree:

> We are here today to honor our dear friend Jim Critchfield. This tree is placed here as a living remembrance of Jim, and for future generations to pause and observe that at one time a great and honorable man, who changed the world, lived among them.
>
> It is fitting that this memorial is placed here in the historic Williamsburg area, the site of so many events that changed the course of our nation's history. Williamsburg was also the home of many of our founding fathers and selfless patriots who gave their all so that we can enjoy the freedom we have today.
>
> Jim Critchfield was a true patriot in the same sense as our founding fathers in that he also was a decorated war hero who fought to protect our country's freedom. Then as a leader in our nation's intelligence service he directed our country's efforts to bring peace and stability to much of Europe and the Middle East. In this latter activity Jim truly was a self-effacing leader (behind the scenes) who made the world a better place for millions of people. His legacy is one that will be remembered and honored as an important part of our nation's history.
>
> We are also here today to show our love and respect to Jim's cherished wife, Lois Critchfield,

who so ably supported and assisted him all these many years.

We all have been blessed having known Jim as a dear friend and neighbor. Our lives have been made richer from the conversations we have with Jim and his unfailing hand of true friendship.

CRITCHFIELD LEGACY

Before closing out this memoir, those who knew Jim well knew he was always writing. He left several papers on subjects that interested him, such as denuclearization, weapons of mass destruction, and a proposal for regional stability in his beloved Middle East. I have appended here what I consider to be the most important and relevant of them. In 2005, I brought them together in a single paper called "Waging Peace". The first paper was written prior to 9/11 and the others were produced periodically after 9/11 up to the winter of 2003. The papers were circulated informally to friends and colleagues, but they were never published. I have shared these essays with many people: journalists, government officials, academics, Arab experts, and Arabs themselves with varying reactions. So it is my pleasure to see them published as part of this memoir. There are nine in total and are presented in chronological order in the Appendix. Perhaps future generations might act upon them. What is that phrase? Never, never give up!

AFTERWORD

America's relations with the rest of the globe may well be determined by the course of events in the Middle East. For more than fifty years, the United States has worked to find a resolution to the conflicts in the region. These efforts have been unsuccessful. If America abdicates its leadership role, then the region of the world between the Eastern Mediterranean and Southeast Asia is likely to sink into decades of chaos and turmoil.

Early into the twenty-first century, James Critchfield asked if a Middle East Treaty Organization was "pie in the sky?" Could such a security organization, which would be firmly committed to freedom of religion and freedom of navigation, take the responsibility for the holy places of the three monotheistic religions and exercise control over important international waterways such as the Suez Canal, Bab el Mandeb, and the Strait of Hormuz? Could the Middle Eastern nations assume responsibility for the first time to develop stable and democratic societies in their own countries?

It can never be too late for these nations to accept responsibility for the future. "It is time for the Arabs to stand together and be counted", he wrote. Together they may have the courage and wisdom to choose a productive future. And the United States, Europe, and Russia should support these efforts.

The nations of the region must get control of the younger generations before their hearts and minds are captured by other forces. They can create modern democratic societies in which terrorists have no place. What Critchfield wrote in October 2001 just after 9/11 is worth repeating here. "It is possible for these nations to restructure the Middle East, including a Palestine state that could live in economic and political comfort with Israel. A wise Israel would embrace such a solution, sharing Jerusalem in some way with the

Islamic and Christian religions. Palestine, Jordan, Syria, and Lebanon could become part of a thriving Middle Eastern economy. If the region remains in turmoil, Israel will eventually be engulfed in a sea of hatred by destructive forces in the area."

America has shown great resolve in working for world peace and stability. Look at the seventy years of US support in Western Europe following World War II, where America showed itself to be a most reliable ally. The current outbreaks of anger and protest in parts of the Middle East against America will dissipate as turmoil and chaos are abated and the region stabilizes. Democracy has never been accomplished in weeks and months. Our founding fathers taught us that.

Lois Critchfield
December 2018 (originally written in 2006)[5]

ENDNOTES

1   The story about this period was told in brother Pat's book in 1986. Richard Critchfield, *Those Days: An American Journey* (New York: Anchor/Doubleday Press, 1986).

2   The CIA Publications Review Board cleared these passages for publication, as required by the Official Secrets Act.

3   A book published posthumously covers this extensively. James H. Critchfield, *Partners at the Creation: The Men Behind Postwar Germany's Defense and Intelligence Establishments* (Annapolis, MD: Naval Institute Press, 2003).

4   The book was published in 2010. *Oman Emerges: An American Company in an Ancient Kingdom by Lois M. Critchfield* (Selwa Press: San Diego, 2010).

5   This final commentary by the author was originally written in 2006 when Waging Peace was finalized. It illustrates how little has changed over the past 12 years and reaffirms that in the Middle East, peace is slow in coming.

APPENDIX

August 20, 2001

A Middle East Treaty Organization?

The Arab-Israeli conflict has resisted all efforts for resolution from within and from outside for more than fifty years. It is, as we enter the twenty-first century, one of the greatest threats to world peace. Are there any lessons of the past century that might apply to the Middle East to make the region between the Eastern Mediterranean and Southeast Asia a safer part of the world in the twenty-first century?

In the three years after the end of WW II, our alliance with the Soviet Union rapidly deteriorated, leaving Western Eurasia strategically an area of high risk to world peace. The North Atlantic Treaty Organization was founded in April 1949, an initiative of President Harry Truman, who was reacting to world events, including two world wars in his lifetime and the rise of two major communist powers. He saw in NATO a military alliance to preserve peace and stability in Europe.

Directly in response to the outbreak of war in Korea in June 1950, President Truman made the decision in September 1950 to make NATO, led by the United States, a defense alliance including a rearmed Germany—a decision that obviously would require the agreement of France, Britain, and the American public. France and Britain immediately rejected the idea; it took another five years of intense negotiation, with German participation starting in 1951, to achieve the agreement of the French. The NATO defense concept fell into place on May 5, 1955, when Germany was accepted into NATO as a sovereign nation. The Soviets reacted quickly; on May 14 the Soviet Union and its communist allies met in Poland to form the Warsaw Pact. Europe became more stable. At the end of the century, Europe was still at peace and moving slowly toward unity.

There are some similarities between Europe in 1949 and the Middle East in 2001. Both had demonstrated an inability to avoid recurring wars. Both demonstrated a dependence on an American presence and leadership. But the purpose of the NATO alliance was to protect its members from an external threat. The purpose of METO would be to protect its members from themselves.

The European nation states had behind them a long history of wars involving interlocking dynasties and competing colonial empires. The idea of a single independent and self-reliant military alliance to maintain peace and stability within all of Europe was never recognized as an option.

The less-well-defined nation states of the Middle East, many of them remnants of European colonialism, may find it easier to seek security and stability in a regional solution patterned on NATO with its half century of success. But many may see METO as a step back toward influence by great powers. But METO would offer a tangible alternative that can be examined and compared with NATO. The United States, because of its history and its postwar record in NATO, seems to be the only candidate to lead a METO. And it will not be easy. Any decisions on the roles of Britain, France, and NATO itself will require careful study. The 1991 coalition is relevant and deserves study.

The idea of testing the Middle East with a formula that was accepted in Europe fifty years ago will probably be rejected out-of-hand by most longtime observers of the Middle East. But what better option is there?

The familiar presence of a US Navy carrier task force in the Mediterranean would be an immediate asset to

META. If the regimes in the region were to accept a version of META and later a Middle East Union as a parallel to the European Union, it would contribute economically to stabilizing Europe, including the Balkans.

During different times in the postwar decades, there have been numerous small political coalitions that have formed and re-formed. Also, every country in the Middle East has had sensitive security understandings with every other country. In such matters, Middle East leaders are remarkably pragmatic.

If an expanded version of METO were to be achieved with Iraq, Iran, and the Arab states of the Gulf and the Arabian Peninsula as members, its impact on Russian interests in Central and Southwest Asia would be a factor.

The fact that the Suez Canal, the Bab el Mandeb at the foot of the Red Sea, and the Strait of Hormuz would all be METO maritime passages would become a central geopolitical factor as world dependence on Gulf oil increases. In the event that a METO were to become a reality, it could be of major significance in the long-term (i.e., 2015–25), when the issue of the global oil supply becomes critical. In other words, a METO of this dimension would probably be a more dramatic and more provocative factor in the twenty-first century than NATO was in the twentieth.

September 15, 2001

A Framework for United States Middle East Policy after September 11

A new policy should address the following:

- Peace and stability in the Middle East should have priority initially focused on the Eastern Mediterranean. Egypt and Israel must be at the center of the new policy.
- The Middle East can extend its influence to the Gulf and to Central and South Asia.
- We must have an organizational framework within which regional cooperation in political and security matters can be brought to a high level.
- If not resolved, the Arab-Israeli conflict must be deemphasized and subordinated to the effort to eliminate terrorism as a major threat to stability and peace everywhere.
- We must increase the role and responsibility of Middle East nations in maintaining stability in their own region.
- We should eliminate or at least reduce necessity for NATO intervention in the region, but cooperation with neighboring NATO states, particularly Turkey, is necessary.

- There must be a strengthening of moderate Islamic forces and a positive image of Islam in the entire region.
- Integral to this policy would be the creation of international laws and a tribunal patterned on the International Military Tribunal created in August 1945 with a constitution, charter and defined crimes of war by terrorism. This can provide the first line of deterrence to terrorism as a method of conducting war.

Required Actions:

- The United States should take the lead in forming a Middle East Treaty Organization in which Israel, Egypt, Jordan, Lebanon, and Syria are members.
- From outside the region, Russia, Britain, and perhaps France should play a direct role. The 1991 coalition might be usefully considered in forming METO.
- This policy should, in the first instance, be discussed with Israel and Egypt; their support and cooperation between them is the key to this proposal.
- The primary purpose of initial discussions with Israel and Egypt is to obtain an agreement that the Arab-Israeli problem has for fifty years been an issue that has had the side effect of encouraging radicalism in many Islamic countries. This is inaccurately described as "Islamic fundamentalism." Achieving cooperation between Israel and Egypt compares with the problem of reconciling French and German attitudes on the defense of Europe in the first half of the 1950s.
- Visible but empty chairs for Iraq and the Palestinians should be put in place by the METO Council. A total abandonment of terrorism should be required before either is seated in METO.

- In a second phase, after a successful organization of METO, membership should be extended to the Arab states of the Peninsula and the Gulf and ultimately to Iraq and Iran.
- A pattern of harboring and supporting terrorist warfare should be identified as sufficient provocation for a response with conventional weapons of war. Establishing rules of engagement for conventional military response to terrorism is a subject on which METO Council policy must be developed.
- METO should as soon as possible assume the role in the Middle East that NATO has in Europe and the Atlantic. The current crisis is contributing to new uneasiness within NATO. The creation of METO would probably contribute to a more stable environment in NATO.

METO offers the Eastern Mediterranean states a way to achieve security. It must be sold to Israel primarily on that basis. Israel may be unwilling to give up its freedom to use modern weapons of war as a response to what are clearly acts of terrorism in Palestinian suicide bombings in Israel. But if terrorism attacks are described as an act of war, a conventional response against the state harboring and supporting terrorism would have a deterrent impact on heads of state who are not themselves prepared to conduct suicide operations.

The Vulnerability and Importance of Iran

It would be a major mistake for the United States to conduct a large and conventional military invasion of Afghanistan, Iran, or Iraq at this time. We should rely on unconventional operations with a strong conventional backup. An unconventional war against Afghanistan should be conducted from the Northern Alliance, Pakistan, and Iran.

If the coalition remains whole, and we avoid a major military operation that could weaken the coalition, Iran will be increasingly vulnerable to both political and military pressures.

The United Sates should make demands on Iran, as it has on Afghanistan, that it end the harboring of terrorists and, as with Pakistan, request support for a US presence in Iran. Specifically it should ask for an Iranian no-fly zone in south Iran. Iran should also be pressed to accept a modest military presence at the Iranian port of Chah Bahar near the Pakistan-Iran border and for an air, rail, and operations base at Zahedan on the Pakistan-Afghan border. Zahedan, as I recall from a visit there some years ago, is a rail center with a line going east into Pakistan and on to Quetta and a line going north to Meshed. Bases for special operations from Zahedan and one or more sites in Pakistan would provide the capability to exert pressure on south Afghanistan and to have opened the possibility of later cooperation with Iran. These operations, combined with those from the Northern Alliance, should be a sufficient force to bring about the capitulation of Afghanistan. The no-fly zone should extend to the entire Iranian coast on the Strait of Hormuz. Presumably, the Sultanate of Oman on the other side of the Strait would collaborate in this strategy, making available its special relations with Iran.

If Russia and significant elements from Central Asia were to cooperate in dealing with the immediate problem of Afghanistan, it may put down the foundation in the entire region that could have far-reaching influence of US and Russian strategic cooperation far beyond the current serous crisis in the Middle East and South Asia.

The United States should probably reveal this strategy sooner rather than later in order to achieve stability in developing the coalition and to weaken the support within the region for the radical elements pursuing policies of terrorism.

We should remember that relations between Iran and Israel were very close in the 1960s. Israel, through Iran, secretly transferred captured Soviet arms to the Yemen regime supported by Saudi Arabia and the British. Iran provided Israel with all of its oil in large tankers shuttling between Iran and Israel. The Turks and the Israelis cooperated in small-arms manufacturing and supply. We will probably see some new small coalitions develop in context of the changing situation in the greater region of the Middle East and South and Central Asia.

The World after September 11

In the fifty-seven years since the use of the atomic bomb to end the war in Japan, I have assumed that proliferation of nuclear weapons would be by nation states and that the head of any nation state would, as a matter of self-preservation, avoid taking the initiative to again use nuclear weapons in war; to do so would run a very high risk of retaliation in kind and an expanding nuclear war. There has in fact been no use of an atomic bomb since Nagasaki on August 9, 1945.

The events of September 11 have radically altered and probably destroyed my optimistic assumption. We must assume that the terrorists who organized the September 11 attack will not hesitate to conduct operations using nuclear or other weapons of mass destruction. The power to precipitate a nuclear war has passed from the nation state to terrorists.

I remained actively involved for thirty years in the region of the world that reaches from Greece in the west to Burma in the east. During much of this time, I was an officer in the CIA and developed relations of mutual trust and professional confidence with individuals in the entire bloc of Arab and other Islamic countries in this region as well as in India and Turkey. Although much of this region remained in continuing turmoil and conflicts in these years, the stable standoff between the Soviet Union and the West led by the United States imposed a real limit on the level and character of violence that developed in these regional conflicts—Arab-Israeli, intra-Arab, Iran-Arab, Pak-India, Greece-Turkey, etc. The end of the Cold War ended the constraints imposed by the very existence of the NATO-Warsaw Pact standoff. The proliferation of weapons of mass destruction and terrorist organizations increased.

The nation states of Europe proved in the first half of the twentieth century incapable of themselves preserving or restoring peace and stability in Europe; two great wars ensued, decisively ending colonial rule in much of the world, including this region. A half-century of peace and stability in Europe required an active role by an Atlantic-Western European alliance led by the United States. History in Europe is repeating itself in the region between the Mediterranean and Southeast Asia.

The region of the world between the Eastern Mediterranean and Southeast Asia is very likely to sink into decades of chaos and turmoil. There are at least five nations in this region that have or could have nuclear weapons. But there are as many nonstate terrorist organizations that have and will have access to weapons of mass destruction.

September 11 shocked the world with evidence that self-preservation is not a constraining factor among significant numbers of educated terrorists. We have for years seen isolated examples of individuals prepared to undertake suicide missions for causes they regard as noble. But on September 11 we saw not only mass suicide but suicide contemplated over months of operational planning and preparation. That has become a characteristic of terrorist operations that must be taken into account. We do not know how far or how deep that fanaticism will be reflected in the forces of nations that harbor and support terrorists.

The nations of this region are collectively moving toward an abyss of chaos and instability that stretches out ahead of all of them for years to come. The terrorist mentality appears to have some appeal to the younger generations. In the Arab and Islamic countries there is a new struggle over control of the hearts and minds of the very populous new generations. We must take it into account in planning military, political, and economic actions in the region. But it is the leaders in these nations who themselves must assume the principal responsibility for education and orientation of their youth.

In my opinion, none of the nations of this region—the Arab states, Israel, Iran, Afghanistan, Pakistan, and India—all creations since WW II, have the wisdom and will to take history-making decisions on the character of the future they collectively face.

The Arab states have, and for a long time can have, the oil wealth to create modern democratic societies in which terrorists would have no place. They could easily restructure the Middle East, starting with the Arab countries, to provide territory and support for a Palestine state that could live in economic and political comfort with Israel. If the Israelis were wise, they would embrace such a solution, sharing Jerusalem in some way with the Islamic and Christian religions. Palestine with Jordan and Lebanon could quickly become part of a thriving Middle East economy. But the Israelis too lack the wisdom and will to contribute to their own security in the future. If the Middle East remains an area of turmoil, Israel will eventually be engulfed in a sea of hatred by destructive forces of the region.

The ineptness of the leaders of the Arab nations of the Eastern Mediterranean over the last half-century gives little reason for optimism about the future. It is they and the leaders of other Islamic nations that must rid their societies of the elements that have captured Islam for their own evil purposes. Outside powers such as the United States, Europe, and Russia cannot accomplish this. Only the state leaders in the Arab countries, Iran, Afghanistan, and Pakistan can do it. Obviously the states of Central Asia also have a stake in this.

The United States can go only so far in uprooting the institution of terrorism that appears to have its origins and source of support in the Middle East. If the region deteriorates into chaos and turmoil, it will be either abandoned or face the anger of an entire world, which will be unlikely to accept permanent turmoil in the region.

This gloomy view of the whole northern littoral of the Indian Ocean is premised on the opinion developed over three decades of shared experiences with the best of the Arab and Islamic colleagues of my own generation. So many of them recognized the need for the nation states of the region to undergo dramatic and perhaps revolutionary change if they were to cope with their problems. It is quite clear that the United States and much of the rest of the world are prepared to go very far in ridding the world of terrorism that seems in its origins endemic to nations of the Middle East and, in its own way, to Israel.

After Afghanistan

After the war in Afghanistan is over and the long process of rebuilding Afghanistan as a nation is being responsibly addressed, the United States will be faced with having a strategy for pursuing the war against terrorism at its center—the Middle East. It must take into account the existence of the holy places of the three monotheistic religions, their institutions, and traditions with very long histories.

The United States should act immediately to cushion off and isolate the Palestine problem—a prerequisite to any innovative initiative in forming a regional security organization with both Israel and Arab participation.

We must do with Israel and the Arab states what was done in Europe in the decade after WW II; we must resolve the bitter conflict between the Arabs and Israel as was done with Germany and its enemies in Western Europe between 1950 and 1955. It was in these years that we formed a defensive alliance against the threat of the Soviet Union and communism. Today the threat is from organized world terrorism with its roots not in Europe but in the Middle East.

With regard to Palestine, the United States would be well advised to set aside the Palestine issue for later resolution after the establishment of a Middle East security organization that can deal with the related problems of terrorism and weapons of mass destruction. The members of such an organization must make a commitment to create a Palestine state under appropriate circumstances and not as an immediate objective. NATO was created in 1949; Germany was accepted as a member only in 1955.

By any standard, the PLO of Yasser Arafat has harbored and supported terrorism as it has been defined since September 11. Osama bin Ladin has probably sanctioned and supported Palestinian operations as the easiest way to influence the Arab-Israeli conflict to serve al Qaeda's own purposes. It is obviously a way to add to the "hate America" component of al Qaeda policy.

For years, the recurring episodes of Palestinian suicide bombing missions in Israel have provoked Israel's response with conventional armed forces attacking Palestinian targets in the West Bank and Gaza. But that has been a small part of the Arab-Israeli conflict in the past fifty years since the creation of Israel. In 1956, Israel joined France and Britain in an attack on the regime of Gamal Abd al Nasser in Egypt, which had taken control of the Suez Canal. Between 1962 and 1968, Israel was a proxy participant in the Yemen War. In 1967 Israel dealt a devastating blow to Egypt, Jordan, and Syria. In the process, Jordan lost the Arab position in Jerusalem and the West Bank. Egypt lost Sinai and the use of the Suez Canal. Syria lost the Golan Heights. The Soviets lost their foothold in Yemen that was held in 1967 by seventy thousand Egyptian forces. Egypt had just introduced chemical weapons into the war in the Yemen. An Egyptian offensive across the Suez Canal in 1973 ultimately led to the canal's recovery and possession of Sinai under a small US monitoring force. In the early 1980s, Arab-Israeli warfare centered in Lebanon, where the United States suffered heavy casualties from several major suicide bombing attacks—probably from terrorism exported from Iran via Syria. The story of violence in the region goes on and on, as do United States efforts to mediate an Israeli-Palestinian peace.

Israel's military power is the result of its own determination to survive in the violent region of the Middle

East. But it is also a part of a long-standing but ambiguously defined Western strategy to rely on Israel in containing the Soviet threat to the Middle East that was, starting in the late 1950s, an integral element in the Cold War.

For two decades after the mid-1950s, the Middle East Arab countries were divided—looking to both Moscow and the West for support and arms. Inevitably, a new round of violence between Israel and the Palestinians has interrupted any progress toward a negotiated Israeli-PLO peace. In recent years many observers have wondered whether it was Osama bin Laden, Yasser Arafat, or someone else calling the shots on another round of violence. Al Qaeda is presumably not interested in seeing a negotiated peace between the Palestinians and Israel. But in his first released statement after September 11, Osama bin Laden had made the Palestine problem one of his major concerns in his war with America.

When the United States launched its massive but conventional air attack on Afghanistan in response to the events of September 11, Israel's response was to send Israeli forces to simply occupy a number of West Bank towns. When President Bush asked that Sharon withdraw these troops, he reluctantly did so. He was testing US policy and wanted to demonstrate to the world that he too had the military power to move against a PLO harboring and supporting terrorism. Someone, perhaps Arafat, perhaps Osama bin Laden, and perhaps Palestinian terrorists harbored by Arafat but controlled by al Qaeda on November 30 significantly upped the ante in terrorist attacks in Jerusalem and Haifa. Sharon interrupted a visit to Washington to hurry home and make a decision on Israel's response.

Most observers in the Middle East see the war with al Qaeda and the Israel-Palestine conflict as firmly joined and an increasingly sensitive element of a new US policy on the region. How does the United States go about isolating the conflict between Israel and the PLO from its ongoing efforts of the United States and the coalition to destroy terrorism at its roots in a number of Middle East countries?

Taking a page out of our history in Europe in the past half century, I have for some time pursued the idea of a Middle East Treaty Organization to provide stability in the region and a framework in which to conduct the war against the related threats of terrorism and weapons of mass destruction. While terrorism constitutes a threat of global dimensions, there is a perception in much of the world that its origins have been in the bloc of nations centered on the Middle East. A primary purpose of a regional security organization would be to destroy operations such as al Qaeda at the source and to inform the world that it is doing so. Since September 11, the Arab and Islamic nations have an image problem that can, in this context, be addressed to the benefit of all.

One of the first tasks facing such an organization would be reaching agreement on the underlying causes of the phenomenon of terrorism that has dominated world news since September 11. This will not be easy. There are deeply entrenched and differing opinions on this issue and how war against terrorism should be conducted. The world coalition that has formed in protest against the September 11 action has only begun to register its influence on a strategy for pursuing the war against terrorism. The wider region of the Middle East and South and Central Asia is now generally recognized as the potentially most unstable and dangerous region in the world.

As a first step, the United States must approach Egypt and Israel to accept and support the idea of a regional security organization modeled on the creation of NATO in 1949 when Western Europe was in disarray. Before doing so, the United States should have British and Russian support. With Israeli and Egypt participation, an approach to Jordan, Lebanon, and Syria might usefully follow. Egypt,

Israel, Lebanon, Syria, and Jordan should be invited to become founding members along with the United States, Britain, and Russia. The initial effort should probably be limited to this small but diverse group. Getting agreement from them may take time. But if success in this first phase is not achieved, the United States would be faced with other far less attractive options. The United States, Britain, and Russia would together probably have enough leverage to make all of this happen. A key issue, of course, is whether any government in Washington will place this much political capital at risk and make the long-range strategic commitment to obtain Israeli support for a dramatically different concept for ensuring Israel's future security, survival, and prosperity.

The conservative Arab states of the Gulf should be offered membership if they agree to fully break with al Qaeda's radical Islamic fundamentalism and agree to support the economic development of the small states at the eastern end of the Mediterranean. Jerusalem must be shared—probably internationalized.

It is possible that a successful conclusion to the US military operation in Afghanistan would have political consequences in the Middle East that would make it unnecessary for the United States to resort to anything comparable to the sustained attacks required to destroy the Taliban regime. If it can be achieved, the initial formation of a Middle East Treaty Organization would go far in bringing the conservative Arabs, Iraq, and Iran to participate in a regional security and development program. I would not expect that fervent opposition to modernization that has been characteristic of the Taliban would, in a Middle East security and economic organization, be a problem.

Fear of future wars, turmoil, and chaos in the region is probably a stronger force in support of a security alliance led by the United States than is widely assumed. At least in the early part of the twenty-first century, the presence of the United States in a leadership role seems likely to remain an element of most international arrangements. The history of the twentieth century strongly suggests that Europe and the greater Middle East will actually look to the United States to remain centrally involved in preserving peace and stability.

I am skeptical that the "hatred of Americans" will, in practical terms, be a problem in the Middle East if our role in regional security is institutionalized. It is also possible that we Americans have learned something about ourselves from the September 11 experience.

My proposed changes in our Middle East policy would involve significant risks to the US government. But the unwanted consequences of not taking these risks may be greater than those involved in taking them. The entire region is loaded with genuine threats to peace and, in various stages of development, with weapons of mass destruction. Instability in the region is endemic. Global terrorism is clearly centered in the region. Population growth in the area is among the highest in the world. Israel's long-term security is at stake. So is that of Palestine. Most of the world's oil is in the Middle East. The communications and transportation lines from Europe, Africa, and Asia all cross in the Middle East. It is an area where our interests and those of Russia may be coming together. All of this adds up to our number one US foreign policy problem. I question whether there is an alternative to the major restructuring described in this paper. This question may remain purely academic. The United States seems inclined to remain with its long-standing policy of cajoling Israel and the Palestinians to return to the negotiating table while we attempt to preserve a working coalition in our continuing war on terrorism in the midst of a shaky world economy. A successful conclusion of our effort in Afghanistan may, of course, generate support for our policy elsewhere in the region.

March 17, 2002

Better Communications as a Deterrent in the War on Terrorism

The northern littoral of the Indian Ocean, stretching eastward from the Eastern Mediterranean and the Red Sea, is the most dangerous area of the world and the center from which the combination of terrorism and weapons of mass destruction threaten nations in all parts of the world. Thomas Friedman's op-ed "A Foul Wind" in the March 10 *New York Times* was depressingly realistic.

Terrorism alone, as we learned on September 11, can move across great oceans and peaceful international borders. But it is the addition of weapons of mass destruction in the hands of terrorists that threatens to produce a chain of reactions that could endanger civilization, as we know it. The United States and other nations sharing this estimate of a worst-case future must communicate more effectively with leaders and people of those nations that harbor terrorism and are engaged in acquiring or already possess weapons of mass destruction.

We are at war. And although this is a new kind of war, a conventional military alliance focused on the Middle East and South and Central Asia is required to protect the nations of this region, not from an external threat but from themselves. A Middle East Treaty Organization, drawing on the experiences with NATO and the defense of Europe fifty years ago, could serve many purposes. Europe too had a history—reaching back more than three hundred years—of being incapable of avoiding ever larger and more violent recurring wars, two of them in the first half of the twentieth century.

In today's world, an initiative by the United States, Russia, and Britain would be a place to start. But the three must impose on Israel and some of the Arab nations responsibility to participate constructively in this regional security organization. Israel and the more moderate Arabs can be brought together as France and Germany were within a NATO that finally fell into place in May 1955.

An International Military Tribunal created by and serving as an instrument of METO, is a requirement that no other international court can meet and satisfy. In most respects, it could be patterned on the International Military Tribunal created in London in August 1945 by the United States, the USSR, Britain, and France.

The Charter for this METO Tribunal must:
1. Explicitly define as war crimes the harboring and supporting of terrorists and the development or possession of weapons of mass destruction.
2. Establish the jurisdiction and competence of this tribunal in dealing with these specific crimes.
3. Empower the tribunal to indict and bring to trial organizations as well as individuals.

This tribunal is necessary as an instrument to bring justice and international law to the region. But its primary and most important purpose would be to improve communications between the US-led coalition and the leaders and the people of all the nations in the region. The principal purpose of carefully planned communications would be to deter those terrorists inclined to resort to the use of weapons of mass destruction and the regimes that harbor and support them.

The tribunal in Nuremberg assembled masses of information and became the most accessible, open, and respected source of information on the individuals, organizations, and events of recent history that were before the court. The legal opinions of the Nuremberg Tribunal ranged far and wide from the narrow legal process of the trial and provided the tribunal with an effective way of communicating with the public and all the parties involved in this complex postwar period. It was mainly these legal opinions and not the formal verdicts of the court that influenced public opinion and had a lasting impact on the character of the Germany and the Europe that emerged in the second half of the twentieth century. After the verdict session on October 1, 1946, the full record was quickly published in a set of fifteen hardback volumes that became part of the public and official libraries all over the world. It also could be found in Germany as a prized personal possession of individuals coping with creating a new and better Germany and Europe. This trial and its record exerted an enormous influence on the postwar history of Germany, Europe, the Soviet Union, and certainly that of the United States. The Nuremberg Tribunal has provided a precedent for an instrument of international justice simultaneously serving as an effective central instrument of communications.

In framing the METO agreement on an international military tribunal, the United States and its coalition partners must assume that it is resorting to principles of international law that were only partially accepted by the Nuremberg Tribunal itself. These principles will be both challenged and used against the United States and other members of METO, but differences and debates over these principles can only enhance the value of the tribunal as a way of improving communications with the public and all the parties involved. If its policies are to have credibility, the coalition against terrorism should be prepared to forego the development and possession of the same weapons of mass destruction that are described in the charter of the METO Tribunal.

Evidence systematically offered by the prosecution would come from open sources, the testimony of witnesses, and classified information released to the court by members of METO. The defendants would have, as they did at Nuremberg, the right of legal defense, but in a forum that does not lend itself to propaganda.

In the six months since September 11, 2001, we have achieved much in Afghanistan while the situation in the Middle East has steadily deteriorated. The Israeli-Palestinian conflict has threatened in the past fortnight to get out of control. I share the view of those who argue that a full resolution to the Israeli-Palestinian problem should be achieved before any major military action against Iraq. A major military operation against Iraq would run a very high risk of interaction with an unsettled conflict between Israel and the Palestinians. It would have a destabilizing impact on Afghanistan. The creation of METO, a METO Tribunal and an imposed solution to the Israeli-Palestinian conflict should precede any military move on Iraq. If there is real progress on these, a major military attack on Iraq may not, at that point, be required.

As a footnote to the above, the way for an indicted leader or regime to avoid being publicly labeled or convicted as a war criminal would be quite simple and clear—to renounce terrorism and the possession of weapons of mass destruction and to accept full international inspection. This is an obvious option open to Iran and Iraq, two candidates for immediate indictment by a METO Tribunal.

The Arab Challenge

It is time for the Arabs to stand together and be counted. President George W. Bush has clearly articulated a policy that harboring and supporting terrorism and possessing weapons of mass destruction will not be tolerated and that those who violate it must accept the consequences.

It is widely accepted that the origins of world terrorism have been primarily in the Arab Middle East. All of the Arabs now approach a moment of decision on their future. The United States has recognized that Saudi Arabia's Crown Prince Abdullah took a historic decision in proposing that all the Arab countries accept the existence of Israel and normalization of trade and diplomatic relations. The proposal was first made during a *New York Times* interview with Tom Friedman on February 17 and later at the March 27–28 Arab summit in Beirut. It came as a surprise to much of the world that Iraq declared its support for Saudi Arabia's initiative. Is it possible that we are at a point in history where all of the Arabs, including Iraq, can expand the wisdom and courage shown in their Beirut decision to create a coalition of Arab nations that is not only at peace with Israel but will be firmly committed to a Middle East free of terrorism and weapons of mass destruction?

President Bush should formally request Saudi Arabia to reconvene the Arab summit in Beirut and confront it with the statement of US policy adopted by the United States after 9/11. Saudi Arabia should be asked to lay before all the Arab nations this momentous historic opportunity to avoid the future of war and instability that lies ahead in the Middle East. Every Arab country should be asked to turn a page in history that will give each of them a new opportunity for peace and stability. Those who do not openly accept these conditions must come away from an Arab summit conference with a clear perception of the consequences of failure to choose a future with a peaceful and productive Arab world.

It is possible that all Arab states, including Iraq, may have the courage and wisdom to choose a productive future; but it is also possible that they may not. The collective positions of the Arab nations will be a major influence on US policy not only in the Middle East but worldwide.

This process of forcing the Arab nations to more openly confront their own future will require time and possibly some political turmoil in their region, but it is a course of action preferable to testing Arab attitudes in an isolated US war against Iraq.

Iran cannot be tested in this way, as it is not an Arab nation. But in asking from the Arabs this review of policy at a summit, the United States should demand of Iran and all other non-Arab nations in the region from the Eastern Mediterranean to South Asia that they remain aloof from this Arab initiative. The collective behavior of the Arabs will obviously influence the future of all nations in the region.

The United States, Great Britain, and Russia should encourage and support the nations attending the Arab summit to take the lead in establishing a Middle East Treaty Organization to include them as founding members. Israel and a Palestine state would become members when it was appropriate and a way could be found to do so. The policy of METO should be focused sharply on the elimination of terrorism and weapons of mass destruction in the Middle East. Its long-term mission would be the fostering of economic stability and growth in the region, including normalization of relations with Israel as clearly spelled out by Crown Prince Abdullah in the first Beirut summit.

From Berlin to Baghdad
(Published as an Op-Ed in the *Wall Street Journal*)

It appears that war with Iraq will be the only option if the threat posed by Saddam Hussein is to be removed. But what comes after a war against Iraq? I was an army officer in Germany when the Second World War ended. After spending more than eight years as a CIA officer in postwar Germany, followed by a longer period with responsibilities in the Middle East, it is my opinion that the occupation of Germany after World War II offers an appropriate model for dealing with a defeated Iraq.

It is often suggested that Iraq should be "liberated, not occupied, and left to develop its own form of democracy." Germany was neither liberated nor left to shape its own future. As with Germany, anything less than unconditional surrender followed by the full occupation of Iraq is unlikely to produce a modern, economically viable and democratic nation. Iraq is unique among the Arab countries. I believe it would react to a firm but constructive policy, including an occupation, in the same way that Germany did. Before Saddam Hussein forcefully took power, Iraq was well on its way to becoming the most modern, well-educated, and progressive country in the Middle East. It still has that potential.

Postwar policy on Iraq should be firmly and fairly executed. Preserving Iraq's integrity within well-defined and announced borders should from the outset be the announced policy of the coalition. The occupying powers must make it clear to Iraq's neighbors—notably Iran and Turkey—that meddling in Iraq's minorities will not be tolerated. Iraq should be preserved as a single state and, like Germany after WW II, evolve step by step as a federation with a central government. From the start the occupying powers must insist on a state in which citizens are Iraqis first and members of a minority second. This will be difficult but not impossible. After all, Germany and France moved toward a pragmatic rapprochement after WW II.

The Ba'ath Party, like the Nazi Party in Germany, should be permanently destroyed. Democratization should start at the village level and move to the national level at the pace and in the pattern followed in forming the German Federal Republic. "Deindustrialization" policy should focus mainly on Iraq's capability to develop and build weapons of mass destruction.

Beyond this, "demilitarization" should concentrate on elimination of the Republican Guard who are guilty of crimes against humanity. Trials of indicted Iraqi war criminals should be open and in accord with international law. As was the case in Germany, the selective rehabilitation of the military should leave room for both officers and enlisted ranks to resume military careers in a reconstituted armed forces under a new and democratic Iraq. It also will be necessary to rehabilitate and use politically acceptable civil servants, technicians, and professionals.

Dealing with the past regime's war criminals isn't easy, and it requires great resolve. In Germany in 1945, the United States was both firm and unambiguous in dealing with ex-Nazis and former military. The German military discharged as POWs simply disappeared into the German population struggling to survive. A much-reported Nazi stronghold of resistance in the Bavarian Alps proved to be a myth. There was no German resistance and virtually no security incidents. The German government was rapidly reestablished up to the level of the individual states in little more than a year after the end of the war.

There are lessons for the success of our postwar Iraq policy that will also ease the concerns of those who anticipate an overwhelming US presence. By early 1946 the responsibility of ridding Germany of the Nazi influences of the past was imposed on the Germans themselves. Without moderating the punitive character of US occupation policy, US Military Government, led by General Lucius Clay, turned major responsibilities for accomplishing US occupation objectives back to the Germans. On September 6, 1946, US occupation policy took a sudden shift from punitive to positive when Secretary of State James Byrnes made it public during a speech before a German audience. In 1949, Konrad Adenauer became the head of a new federal German regime with an elected parliament. But at the same time, the formal occupation was preserved. In the six years that followed, NATO and the Western European Union took form. On May 5, 1955, the occupation ended. West Germany, primarily under US influence, became a democracy, a solid ally of the United States within NATO and the economic driving force within a stable and prosperous Western Europe. Fifty years of peace and stability in Europe followed.

Of course, I am not suggesting that Iraq and Germany are comparable in themselves—either in terms of their history as nation-states, or in terms of their political and cultural aspirations. What I do believe, however, is that we face a comparable opportunity, post-Saddam, to play the role of benevolent but not disinterested rebuilder. I was there in 1945, and I hear the echoes of the moment today.

The Changing Character of War

Two developments late in World War II, one in Europe and the other in Japan, caused me to think about the changing character of war. I have continued to reflect on these for more than fifty years and am only now in 2003 putting some of my thoughts on paper. The conscious decision by the British to resort to massive bombing of German cities, including Dresden and Hamburg, with the intent to persuade the Germans to shorten the war, was a dramatic change in the character of war. Even more dramatic, the United States attacking large Japanese cities with two atomic bombs to end the war in the Pacific had moved the world into the era of nuclear war.

Changes in the character and rules of land warfare in the American Civil War, World War I, and World War II came largely from new weapons technology. But these were limited mainly to individual- and crew-served weapons. The enormous expansion of air and naval weapons systems in World War II was largely incremental and only added to the options to nations at war within established rules. Massive bombing of cities and the introduction of nuclear weapons raised new questions on morality and the rules of warfare. But neither Britain nor the United States has been anxious to put these changes in warfare into an international perspective.

In the past fifty years, many nations have acquired at least a limited capability to bomb the civilian population of cities in other countries. And there has been a steady proliferation of nuclear weapons. The strategic standoff between the Soviet

Union and the United States produced a worldwide unwritten understanding that regional wars could not be extended to the use of nuclear weapons or mass bombing of civilian populations. Although many nations know that sooner or later the British bombing of Dresden and American atomic attacks on Hiroshima and Nagasaki must be placed in context of modern war. But there has been no consensus in the United Nations Security Council or any other international forum to undertake this sensitive task. Thus, the constraint on any significant increase in the violent character of war is solely a matter of conscience and wisdom of the individual leader possessing weapons of mass destruction.

To many of us who experienced World War II and have reflected on the potential for chaos on a regional war going out of control, Iraq is the source of very deep anxiety. It is so because the constraint imposed by the United States and Soviet standoff is gone. I am fearful that there may be national leaders who may feel they have a license to change the rules of warfare, as the Western Allies did late in World War II. It is possible, although certainly not probable, that war in Iraq could produce a chain reaction of conflict. But it is also quite possible that there are men in Iraq who recognize this danger, and will not permit Saddam Hussein to take the first fateful step of launching chemical or biological weapons of mass destruction in the narrow confines of the Middle East. I am sufficiently optimistic that a war in Iraq will be limited.

Postscript: The invasion of Iraq began on March 20, 2003. Baghdad fell on April 9, 2003. On May 1, 2003, President Bush declared the "end of major combat operations." The Ba'ath Party was driven from power and Saddam Hussein removed from office. Saddam Hussein was captured on December 14, 2003.